RATTLESNAKES ON THE FLOOR

A Successful Life
on the
Schizophrenic Spectrum

For Sara,
With warm wishes for the rest of the cold winter!
E. Kirsten Peters

Dr. E. Kirsten Peters

OTHER BOOKS BY THE AUTHOR

Under the pen name "Irene Allen"

Quaker Silence – Villard Books/Random House

Quaker Witness – Villard Books/Random House

Quaker Testimony – St. Martin's Press

Quaker Indictment – St. Martin's Press

Under own name

No Stone Unturned – W.H. Freeman

Geology from Experience (with Dr. Larry Davis) – W.H. Freeman

Planet Rock Doc – Washington State University Press

The Whole Story of Climate – Prometheus Books

In memory of my parents

and with thanks to Nils, Krista and Mary

AUTHOR'S NOTE:

The events related in this book are all factually accurate. The names of mental patients, some psychiatrists and certain friends have been changed to protect their privacy.

Table of Contents

AUTHOR'S NOTE: iv
PROLOGUE 1
CHAPTER 1: GETTING STARTED 6
CHAPTER 2: RETURN TO PRINCETON 28
CHAPTER 3: HARVARD YEARS 49
CHAPTER 4: BOOKS AND GEOLOGY 74
CHAPTER 5: PROGRESSION OF THE DISORDER 102
CHAPTER 6: A NEW DIAGNOSIS 124
CHAPTER 7: TRICKS OF THE TRADE 154
CHAPTER 8: FINAL DIAGNOSIS 180
CHAPTER 9: REFLECTIONS 208
ACKNOWLEDGMENTS 216

PROLOGUE

Each morning, a staff member gathers together those of us who are behaving well. Her task is to give us the opportunity to exercise outside the confines of the locked psychiatric ward. Exercise has always been a way for me to cope with the inner intensity of my life-long mental illness, so the chance to move around and work up a sweat is highly important. I smile and nod at the staffer, hoping I can go with her to a different part of the hospital.

In a little group, we who have been so fortunate as to be selected, pass through the heavy door to the ward, with its buzzer and automatic locking mechanism. That door separates our special part of the hospital from the rest of the world. From there, we take a nearby elevator and walk a short distance down a hall.

Two small rooms, each with windows on one side, await us. The first has a couple of treadmills and a rowing machine in it. The second room has a hardwood floor and is set up for shooting baskets. The staff member who oversees our efforts at exercise doesn't act as a coach or personal trainer, but is simply tasked with the job of making sure we don't threaten one another or behave too strangely. The problematic patients have been left behind in the locked ward, so those of us in the modest exercise rooms never cause anyone trouble.

The basketball area is my favorite place in the hospital. The little room is small enough that a loose ball doesn't have far to go before it hits a wall and starts to return toward the center of the space. I have arthritic knees, and I can't run after a loose basketball on a standard-sized court, but even I can retrieve balls in the small room. Other mental patients sometimes join me, and we all shoot hoops amicably. Playing with others is a pleasure but, as it happens, one time I am all by myself in the basketball room for several days in a row.

I'm not sure exactly when it starts, but there comes to be an otherworldly and uplifting experience in that small room as I shoot hoops. Although I may be alone from the point of view of the hospital staffer in charge, I strongly feel the presence of several marvelously joyful people around me as I dribble and shoot the ball. I don't literally see anyone else on the hardwood floor, but at a visceral level I feel surrounded by wonderfully supportive teammates. Better still, it seems quite evident there is a section of bleachers on one side of the room. The bleachers are packed thickly with the same type of people on the floor with me. They cheer me onward not as a basketball player, which isn't important to me, but as a hard-pressed person trying to meet the great challenges of deep illness in a psychiatric ward.

Perhaps because the room is so small, the bleachers stand beyond the solid wall beside the backboard. That location would be a problem for a normal audience. But for the good souls sitting in the bleachers, a sheetrock wall is no hindrance to being profoundly and completely with me every minute I am allowed in the basketball room.

The joyful people in the bleachers greatly outnumber those on the hardwood floor, and they come to define the whole experience of shooting baskets during my hospital stay. The people packed onto the bleachers are what I might term a chorus of angels, beings who keep me company and guide me resolutely forward during some terribly difficult days. I am sometimes in excruciating mental pain, and, therefore often suicidal. Beyond all that, I am suffering strongly with the side-effects of psychiatric drugs that are being pushed on me in high doses by the medical system in which I am enmeshed. But my joyful audience in the basketball room helps sustain me through the great suffering that engulfs me during that sojourn in the psych ward.

As my time in the hospital draws to a close, I lose the close connection I feel with the uplifting people in the basketball room. On my last day for exercise, I stride into the room and instantly realize the chorus of angels have become so distant I can almost no longer feel their presence. I don't have miraculous teammates around me on the hardwood floor, and my separation from the special people in the bleachers hurts me keenly.

Going quickly over to the wall beyond which the packed bleachers should be located, I feel my way forward with an outstretched hand. I hope the wall is permeable, something I can pass through to get to where the mass of wonderful people was located. I want to leave my dark world behind and join the good souls in those bleachers, gladly exchanging the confines of my life and its episodic psychiatric suffering for the company of the angelic beings.

My outstretched hand encounters solid sheetrock, unlike the hoped-for permeability. Visceral disappointment hits me as the nerves in my hand register the cool and solid wall. It is staggering to realize I am cut off from the joyous people I have known so well. In desperation, I move my hand upward, trying to draw the curtain of reality away from the wall, hoping against hope there is still some way for me to rejoin the souls I have come to know beyond the gypsum boards. When that doesn't work, I try to scratch my way through the wall with my fingernails.

At one level, I know my efforts make no sense. I hold a doctorate in physical science from Harvard University, and I often can organize my thoughts and reason quite well about facts. My logical part tells me to stop scratching at a solid part of the hospital building. But at a much deeper level, I desperately want to get through the wall and rejoin the invisible people, so for a while, I continue to run my fingernails across the sheetrock, hoping I somehow can breach the wall. In time, of course, I have to accept that I cannot escape the confines of the room, I am alone in the little basketball court, a deeply ill and strongly suffering patient who has no chorus around her any longer.

That night, as I lie on the old and lumpy mattress of my hospital bed, I contemplate my pending discharge and look back at my last experience in the basketball room. Part of me is shocked I was so ready to leave my life entirely behind – for I gladly would have done so in an instant if I could get through the wall beyond which those amazing bleachers seemed to stand. I would have left my identity, my work, my family, my church, and all my friends. In short, I would have traded absolutely everything I know and love for a chance to join those whose presence I had so strongly felt.

For weeks after my discharge from the hospital, I longed for the people in the bleachers. As I lie awake in bed at night at home, I recall them to memory again and again, wondering if I will ever experience them once more. Longing for them keeps me awake with a soulful desire, and in time, my memories of the people in the bleachers are worn at the edges from my frequent handling of them.

No mystical nor psychotic experience earlier in my life was like what I knew in the basketball room, and I want to be back even for one hour on the hardwood floor of the court with my invisible friends still so profoundly and clearly with me. I even consider returning to the hospital at night to pick the lock on the exercise room door, so strong is my desire to be reunited with those I'd known briefly but intensely. Although time eases the depth of my loss, I still feel alone when comparing my life in the regular world to the richest communions I enjoyed while shooting hoops as a psychiatric patient.

The question I've been left with in recent times is how to think about the joyful people beyond the wall of the basketball room. Should I ascribe to them meaning and, if so, of what in particular? Or do I dismiss them as mere products of stupefying illness or rapid medication changes?

Some professionals in the mental health industry see the people in the bleachers as a delusion, perhaps enhanced by the energy of a manic state. My current psychiatrist, whose opinion I seek on the matter, sees my chorus of angels as an element of psychosis in my disease. Perhaps she is right from her perspective, but I find her answer to my questions strangely unsatisfying, even adopting her worldview. What, I now wonder, is the meaning of psychosis? What am I really to make of the oddest yet most powerful and uplifting experiences I have ever known?

I will continue to ponder what I came to know beyond the solid wall of the exercise room. Maybe someday, no doubt strongly ill, I'll return to that small basketball court as a patient. God willing, perhaps, I'll walk through the solid sheetrock next time, like the children in the tales of C.S. Lewis who pass so quickly through the back of the wardrobe and spring into Narnia. Of course, I don't expect that will be possible – I am rational most of the time. But I do hope and pray I might somehow rejoin the chorus of angels I came to know. Perhaps the special beings are for me, a foretaste of heaven. When I entertain that thought, it helps take the sting out of death – not a bad result of a psychotic experience during a terribly difficult time.

When I mull over my experiences in and out of hospitals, it's clear that a few of us are drafted against our will, put into uniforms, and sent to the very frontiers of the mind. We fight complex battles with illness and drugs and sometimes with the doctors. The lucky among us return home, naturally the worse for wear, but still ambulatory. In that sense, I'm deeply fortunate and grateful for it. When the world gives us battered veterans a safe place to rest as we rebuild, we can often heal sufficiently that we can pass for normal, occupying ourselves with the ordinary tasks of daily life outside institutions. But it's also true that those of us who serve on the unpredictable frontier, never forget where we have been, and what happens to us when we are there.

CHAPTER 1:

GETTING STARTED

I've never been a fan of horror movies. Perhaps that's because a few times when I was in middle school, I heard something like maniacal laughter imprinted over every day sounds. I well remember drawing myself a bath and hearing such laughter obliterating the sound of running water falling from the faucet into the bathtub. I was confused and frightened by the experience. Another day, I heard the rising and falling tones of maniacal laughter as I turned on the water to fill the bathroom sink. Why simple plumbing sounds triggered the insane laughter, I surely couldn't say. But those sounds in my childhood were deeply alarming, filling my head in just an instant, maddening me no matter how I tried to turn away from them. Because maniacal laughter was my first auditory hallucination, my memory of it remains fresh. The intense laughter was frightening to experience, and such hallucinations still make me afraid even though I am used to them.

The maniacal laughter in the bathroom disturbed me enough that I mentioned the experiences to my pediatrician when I was in my early teens. It was clear from his face he didn't like what I was trying to describe.

"If that keeps up, young lady, you'll have to see a psychiatrist," he said tersely.

As a small-town kid with no family history of medical intervention for mental illness, I actually didn't know what a psychiatrist was. But that the pediatrician was afraid of what I was reporting, that much was clear.

It's no wonder that when I started to hear what I can only term messages – sharp on-and-off sounds like Morse code signals – I didn't mention them to anyone. With just a dash of reflection, I knew that "hearing things" was something only crazy people did, and I didn't want to be crazy. The pattern of my privacy about what I heard was something to which I often reverted in the years and decades that followed. Unfortunately, because of such early experiences, youngsters all too often make decisions that shape far too much of what is to come. Silence becomes the norm as they stumble along trying both to adapt to mental illness and resist it as best they can.

There were other, and actually more difficult, childhood experiences. Much earlier, when I was a little girl, I had to endure strong night terrors. While many kids are afraid of the dark, my fears were extreme. To be sure, the general process of going to bed each night had its emotionally reassuring points because my father often read to my brother and me as we settled down for sleep. But, of course, being put to bed always ended with my brother going to his room and me to mine, followed by my parent turning out the lights. That left me alone in the dark in my small bedroom with its slanting ceiling, with only my terror for a companion.

Not surprisingly, I often got up again and sought out the company of my parents, sometimes in tears. Seeing that my fear was real and not some simple delaying tactic about going to bed, they comforted me as best they could. My mother, in particular, was always in tune with her children, and I think she knew something of how much I suffered. But my parents simply couldn't understand how deeply, if irrationally, afraid I was when they returned me to bed and turned off the light in my room once more.

A nightlight provided a little bit of relief from my fears, and I kept my eyes fixed on the light plugged into the outlet across the small room from me. But knowing that a greater darkness surrounded the whole house created a roaring terror in my mind. Even though I didn't believe in ghosts and had no reason to fear criminals lurking in the backyard, my stomach was tied up in knots as I kept my eyes on that little nightlight.

Again and again, I crept downstairs where my parents were reading or watching television, only to be gently but firmly returned to bed. My father, a kind man, said he understood the alarm inspired by "the dark at the head of the stairs," that fear of the unknown we all sometimes feel. I think he understood part of what I felt, but not the chasm of dread that often enveloped me when I was – quite objectively – safe and sound.

As a small girl, I was also deeply afraid of school. I liked the lessons we learned, and I got along with my classmates and the teachers. But I was so painfully shy that school was a daily torture. Kindergarten, first and second grade, all were laced with stomach pain from the stress of heading into the classroom group. I often pleaded in tears with my mother that I stay home with her. She understood I was truly suffering, and at least once she came to my grade school to discuss my distress with my teacher and the principal. The adults could find nothing amiss in my classroom, and I couldn't explain what was wrong. While many kids sometimes feel shy or express fears about school life, I was clearly pained to an unusual extent. But, because I was a well-brought-up and compliant kid, I did as I was directed and went to school whenever my mother wouldn't let me stay home. In first grade, there really isn't much choice about the matter.

Still, my childhood had wonderful elements mixed in with fear and suffering. I was raised in Pullman, Washington, a small town near the border with Idaho, home to Washington State University. Small town life in the rural Northwest has many virtues, and I benefitted from them all in abundance. Whenever the weather was fair and we were not in school or at church, my brother and I played outdoors with the neighborhood kids. We lived on a dead-end street and could ride our bikes or roller skate up and down the blacktop in front of the house and on the sidewalk across the street from our home. I walked to and from the local elementary school with my neighborhood friends on school days. Because we lived half a block from the campus of WSU, my companions and I had large lawns and hills on which to run in the summer and sled in the winter. Some Saturdays, we scoured the campus for soda pop bottles that we redeemed for nickels at a nearby grocery store.

Our parents did not oversee our playtime hours, so my friends and I amused ourselves along any of the lines our imagination dictated, a blessing for which I've been grateful ever since. In the summers, we were outside, throwing raw eggs over the house and marveling that they were intact when they landed in the lawn. When the weather was poor, I invented board games from scratch that we played for hours.

Occasionally, there were treats of another type. One of my good friends at school was a daughter of a farmer. Staying over at her house, we could ride the family's patient and calm farm horse up and down the gravel roads near her home. In fifth grade, the whole class had the adventure of going together to a camp in the woods for a week. There we could imagine we were doing something romantic and almost dangerous, while in fact, we were as safe as possible.

But I suspect my early childhood was woven together with strong strands of pleasure simply because my home life was good. My parents were good to my brother and me. My mother defined herself as a homemaker, but she had a bachelor's degree and talked to us kids seriously. She made bread and wove fabric, but also read seriously and belonged to book clubs. My father held a Ph.D. and was a faculty member in the Political Science (or Government) Department at WSU. In a nutshell, my brother and I had two parents who read to us at bedtime and taught us all they could. Choosing one's parents wisely is worth the world, especially if you are destined for life-long mental illness.

I think growing up in a stable home is the single most important variable that gives you a chance of surviving into middle age. I'm sure that in my case, habits of life established by the time I was seven or eight years old, help me today as I find my way forward through round after round of debilitating hospitalizations and more minor but still disruptive episodes of crippling mental states.

I'm fortunate that as an adult I can research my own illness and treatment options, an ability that piggybacks on my lifelong habit of intense reading. Daily, serious reading is an approach to living I learned well before my tenth birthday. And although I learned to read at school, I'm sure I deeply valued books in large measure because my parents cherished them. My mother made sure my brother and I were registered as users at our public library, and when we roamed around in the summers on foot or on our bicycles, one common destination was the town library. My brother and I did well in the summer reading program there – which consisted largely of construction-paper symbols with our names on them that marched through a series of steps, one for each book we read.

Because Nils was four years my senior and I looked up to him, I was influenced by his choice of books. When he started a phase of reading the Encyclopedia Brown detective stories, I followed suit. Ditto for the science fiction of Isaac Asimov and a zillion Agatha Christie mysteries. As my young life unfolded, I read above my grade level in large measure because my home life strongly promoted daily reading well beyond school requirements.

From my viewpoint now, the books I devoured had significant literary limitations, but for a fourth or fifth-grader, they were a serious way of using free time, contributing to both basic reading skills and general knowledge of the world. By the time my brother Nils was too old to share anything he read with his much younger sister, my habits had been formed, and reading remains something I do each day when I'm not actually so ill that I'm hospitalized.

Even television in our household was significantly educational. Watching the evening news was a nightly ritual for the whole family, with the four of us gathering together and my father explaining the background and significance of the stories to my brother and me. As a family, we watched the first landing on the moon, with my father making sure we understood how historic the day was by taking photographs of the television screen with his 35 mm camera.

As the Watergate scandal unfolded, Nils and I also learned at home about the constitution and the separation of powers. In the summer of 1973, when I was 13, our family television time was dominated by daily coverage of the Senate special committee chaired by Senator Sam Ervin as he and his colleagues investigated the activities of Richard Nixon's staffers and campaign workers. The following summer, Texas Rep. Barbara Jordan of the House impeachment committee held us spellbound as her deep, booming voice helped the nation understand the constitutional issues behind the headlines. As always, I'm sure our family discussions solidified what I learned.

I don't know whether my parents consciously chose to raise their children as miniature intellectuals, or if our family life simply reflected how they wanted to spend their evenings. But in any event, something in me caught fire due to the sparks given off by the Watergate hearings, by Isaac Asimov, and by the other parts of my daily childhood life. Not many of my friends were so hell-bent on learning about abstractions as I was before we hit high school. If there's a bell curve of simple but sustained intellectual energy, I fell pretty far along toward one end, taking full advantage of what my family and school environment could give me.

But mixed with all those good experiences of childhood centered on learning were the inner pains that seemed to afflict me far too often and too deeply. My life was fundamentally incoherent and confusing from that perspective. Yet, as a kid, all one can do is accept the world as it is and cope with it from day to day. And, of course, children have no way of knowing what parts of their evolving internal experiences are inherent in growing up and which parts may have other significance. I was a serious and thoughtful kid, I suspect, but I was as clueless as the next youngster about what to make of my inner life.

As it happened, the first clear tsunami of changes puberty brought to my internal experience was surprisingly positive. Quite out of the blue, somewhere in my middle school years, I had several mystical experiences. They were, of course, arresting, and could have been disorienting from that perspective. But because the inner excursions were centered on a profound sense of peace and well-being, I certainly had no complaints about what in that era we might have called natural "trips."

Pretty much by definition, mystical experiences cannot be captured in words. But feelings of a wonderful warmth enveloping everything, of the sense that simple inanimate objects reflect the divine, or of a glorious inward light illuminating all – such experiences were not something anyone could possibly dislike or want to avoid. Still, it may have been vaguely disquieting to me that such episodes were not something people around me talked about. I discussed them once with my father, and he and I agreed that religious life best described the experiences.

But, as it happened, our denomination – situated in the lower ranks of Protestantism – didn't provide a way to further digest the events. Protestants generally emphasize the written words of scripture and don't celebrate mystical life. So, although I carefully stored my experiences in my memory, I didn't know what to make of them. They likely made me more deeply interested in religious life than I otherwise would have been, but I couldn't take any next steps in my understanding of what I experienced until years had passed.

Looking back, I can see that the darker aspects of my inner life were tied up with religious experience, too. As one example, starting at some point in middle school, I had a remarkably strong interest in a particular gospel story most young people probably don't pay any attention to. Like some other parts of the gospels, the story occurs in basic form in more than one book.

My favorite version is in Mark. A short but pithy passage explains that a man was living apart from everyone else, among the tombs. The man spent his time "crying, and cutting himself with stones." In short, he was the picture of mental illness, as we would call it now. Jesus heals the man in the story, cleansing him of what the scriptures call spirits. But what was significant to me, what stuck with me so strongly, was not the healing itself. Instead, it's the verse before Jesus makes the man whole, the one in which he asks the possessed man his name. The wretched man replies, "My name is Legion, for we are many," a reference to the many unclean spirits within him.

I can't remember clearly when it happened, but the day came when I felt 'Legion' was my true name. I seemed to be more like the man in that story than the people around me. Throughout my adult life, I've continued to identify with Legion – that is, with the deeply unwell man before he is healed. Indeed, during my most recent time in a locked psychiatric ward, I read Mark's account of the Legion story aloud to my minister when she visited me. She directed my attention to the idea that Jesus related to the man not just when his illness tormented him, but after he was healed, as well. But although the Rector is a wiser and more faithful woman than I, and although she can read the story in Greek, I felt sure she was somehow missing the point. What grips me is the first part of the tale, not the second. It's a simple but significant truth that some of us have fractured minds, made up of legions of pieces, fragments that jostle together and stir up great pain. When we first meet Legion in the story, he is profoundly unwell, and he suffers terribly because of it. That simple but rich image either speaks to you or it doesn't, and I remain deeply impressed by how much it has meant to me from my teen years onward into retirement.

One thing my home church did well was teaching me a fair amount of scripture, both of the Old and New Testament. My fellow Sunday school classmates and I memorized the order of the books of the Bible, knowledge quite useful if you want to look something up in a bound copy of the Good Book or to keep track of where your favorite passages are printed. We learned some psalms by heart, and of my own accord, I added some of the prophets' most radical verses. Because we heard some passages of the Bible so many times in Sunday morning worship services, we had at least a passive knowledge of many portions of scripture, especially the gospel stories and parables.

While my early mystical experiences in middle school were both positive and interesting, and while my family life remained good, as I moved further into my teen years, peace and well-being simply disappeared. By the last two years of high school, I started to slip into some problematic experiences. Bit by bit it came to feel as if life was a hike up a steep hill, rather than a walk on level ground. I started to sleep less, and I felt the normal pains of life more keenly. The changes didn't make much sense. The outward conditions of my life were good – and I realized at least that much.

What could be wrong, I wondered? I had many friends at school, including a couple of high school boyfriends to go with to movies and passionately kiss, and I excelled in all my classes. Like other bright kids in some of the public schools of this country, I did become bored by my senior year. But I channeled my energies into activities no worse than taking a couple of classes at WSU and working part-time washing dishes in a steamy cafeteria kitchen on campus.

At some point in high school, a friend asked me if I was registered to take the SATs. I was not, so blissfully isolated was I from anxiety about the college application process. I discovered that I could quickly register by paying a penalty and sit for the exams on an upcoming Saturday. I took the tests with a minimum of stress, a fact that may have helped my performance. When my results arrived in the mail, my verbal and math scores were exceptionally high, in keeping with my straight-A high school grades.

My parents had raised me to value academics, and my older brother had already blazed a highly successful path through a private liberal arts college where he had done well as a chemistry major. I was progressing well on a similar track and should have been pleased. But as my senior year in high school progressed, I felt worse and worse. Insomnia became a close companion that kept my mind in a fog during the day and prevented sleep the following night. Because my mind refused to settle down at bedtime, I assumed it was worry that kept me awake. I was uneasy, I told myself, although I didn't know about what.

At times I thought my growing troubles were, perhaps, simply what adult life was going to be like. Maybe all grown-ups felt like I did, confused about what ailed them even while they suffered deep, daily unease. In that case, my best response was surely to soldier on, something that my Scandinavian heritage seemed to recommend to me as a general answer to pain.

There was also another source of suffering that ever so gradually crept up on me during my last year of high school. I had always been an active girl, loving outdoor activities, walking for miles, and enjoying P.E. class in an era when many girls thought it unladylike to do jumping jacks. But bit-by-bit, I started to experience low-level but significant pain in my muscles and around my joints after exercise. Because the transition came so slowly, I just adapted to it, thinking it was normal. The pain to which I was adapting in high school was quite real, but because I didn't acknowledge it to others it occupied a phantom-like status in my life, both vividly present yet shadow-filled. As with my emotional suffering, I thought the best answer I could make to the physical aches in my muscles and around my joints was to deny the pain and continue as if nothing were wrong.

But it was my mental suffering that was much more significant. When I tossed and turned at night it wasn't my body, but my mind, that tormented me. I couldn't fathom my internal unease, nor why it was growing in pitch as high school started to wind down. True, getting ready to leave home for college was coming squarely into view. Sometimes I thought the upcoming separation from my family kept me awake at night. But the idea didn't appear to explain much, as I had always looked forward to going to a university, the expected next-step in life for me.

Nevertheless, as insomnia became a chronic part of my life and I felt increasingly poorly, I talked to my family about not going to college the fall after high school. I just didn't feel up to it, I tried to explain. My parents and brother, however, told me I simply had a case of cold feet. I would feel better when I was established on my own as a college student, with new friends around me and new academic challenges I doubtless would enjoy. I wanted to believe all that, and I simply didn't have the life-experience to contest my family's prediction.

As it happened, there was a girl in my high school who had been a grade ahead of me. She was an amazingly smart and emotionally mature young woman whom I admired. She had left our hometown and gone Back East to Princeton University. She came home at Thanksgiving and happened to talk to a friend and me. Although she had been at Princeton for only two months, she sung its praises. I didn't follow all she said, and I'm sure I didn't have the faintest idea where the university in question actually was. But with the compelling logic of teenage life, I knew that I wanted to be like Amy. Perhaps I could become more like her if I went to her college – so why not apply to Princeton?

In the end, I applied to Princeton and three other colleges around the nation. I was admitted to all but one of the schools. Princeton offered me the most significant scholarship of the institutions that wanted me. My parents would still have to contribute to my bills, but they clearly felt that, with some sacrifices, they could swing their part of the deal. Although I still felt deeply uneasy about my internal states and my nightly failure to sleep well, it seemed the train of my life was leaving the station known as home. Everyone around me was saying I should get on board, and I came to think I had no choice about the matter. So off I went.

The fall of my freshman year at Princeton made it abundantly clear that the institution would offer me many intellectual challenges. It was equally apparent I could revel in them all. Academic doors opened in the Ivy atmosphere that simply had been beyond my ken in the public high school of my small hometown. I started to study intensely, and I learned for the first time how to begin to master much greater swaths of knowledge than I had ever addressed in my youth. My favorite classes were philosophy and religion, courses in which even as freshmen, students wrote frequent papers expressing our ideas and arguments. But I also liked economics and German. All my classes were intoxicating and exciting. In that way, at least, Princeton was built for me.

I soon started to feel at home in Princeton's main library, where I spent a great deal of time. It's located in the old part of campus. The stone buildings, ivy covered walls, and stone sidewalks around the library all impressed me. At times I was quite intimidated by everything about Princeton. But at a dim level I also knew that compared to some of my freshman classmates, I truly belonged at the university. I had not enrolled to get ahead in the world, to meet the right people for a career on Wall Street, or to marry a millionaire's son. I was simply in college to expand my mind as much as I could, believing that education would be its own reward.

In a nutshell, I was truly an idealistic young person, trusting my whole life to abstractions like education, to the long and hard hours of study that gave me the reliable internal pleasures of learning. During my good days, I knew that a measure of the Ivy tradition appealed to the most vital part of what made me and some other students tick. So, I dug into the university's resources, and in short order, I became known to several faculty members and teaching assistants in the philosophy and religion departments. They seemed to value the intense and hard-working young woman who had washed up in New Jersey from a part of the country they had never heard about, somewhere in the far-off rural Northwest.

To be sure, the Ivy atmosphere in which I was immersed had some peculiar aspects that meant I would never feel fully at home at the university. Quite a number of undergraduates in my day were from wealthy families, a few from the richest stratum of our society including the Rockefeller and Ford dynasties. On my first day at the dorm, I arrived with two mismatched hand-me-down suitcases, along with a manual typewriter in a cardboard box. As I was looking around near the front door of the building, a black limousine rolled up to the curb. Out of it stepped a young scion starting his collegiate career. The limousine's chauffeur, complete with uniform and dark cap, helped the young man unload the many pieces of gear he felt necessary to bring to college. Later that fall, a boy down the hall from me in the dorm got a delivery of champagne for his 18th birthday celebration, a gift sent to him by his father. While it's true that the legal drinking age in New Jersey was 18 at the time, what was remarkable to a hayseed like me was that any father would send champagne to his son on the occasion of a birthday.

It also became clear that many of my prep school counterparts had already travelled around Europe. My typical family trips had been to places like the plains of Saskatchewan where we visited relatives. But, as I was to find again and again, one wonderful aspect of Princeton was that the faculty treated the wide range of students enrolled at the university very much the same. We were on a level playing field in the classroom, and what mattered was who could excel. I could do exactly that, and I reveled in the new intellectual vistas my college life began to show me.

Still, I was acutely homesick all fall. My stomach hurt deeply as I longed for the Northwest. I missed my family most strongly, of course, but I also missed the kids I had grown up with. My hometown was small, so I knew everyone in my high school graduating class to one extent or another. I knew a number of my friends' parents, having been in their houses or because my parents knew them from church or other connections. Finding myself 3,000 miles away from everyone I knew well was deeply painful.

Beyond feeling the absence of a lot of good people in my life, I also missed the cold, dry, and clear air of the inland Northwest and the smell of ponderosa and tamarack in the hills and buttes. And as a teenager, I missed the simple pleasures of rural life, like gunning a pickup truck down a gravel road with the windows open and country music blasting from the radio. There were no National Forests at the edge of Princeton, let alone range land so empty it could make you imagine you were back on the frontier of the nineteenth-century West. While I marveled at all the people crammed into New Jersey, I deeply missed the wide sky and infinite spaces of the country I knew well. In short, I was a long way from home, and I felt it keenly.

Enrolling at Princeton had taken a splash of courage for an underexposed and tormented girl like myself. One activity I volunteered for the first fall I was there also required me to use the most adventuresome part of my personality. It was a simple fact that the cost of attending the university – even with scholarship aid – was high. As a responsible young woman, I was impressed by what my parents had to pay for my education. As it happened, Princeton had a physical education requirement for students, and one way of earning a semester's P.E. credit was to take an ROTC class and drill with the unit on Saturdays. The ROTC class wouldn't in itself obligate me to the Army, but if I were interested in later going that route the program would pay all my bills for my remaining time at Princeton. I had significant misgivings about the military, mostly because I suspected it contradicted my church values. But I reasoned that the way to learn something about the Army was to spend time in the ROTC unit, learn a bit about military life, and get acquainted with the enlisted personnel and the officers who manned the program. College should be about broadening one's horizons, after all, and the way to learn most about a part of the world that's simply foreign to you and your family is to immerse yourself in it. So, I signed up for ROTC class.

During the week we ROTC freshmen met for lecture classes that gave us a basic introduction to the organization and history of the Army. On select Saturdays, we met for longer periods of time. We needed to wear uniforms for those events, so a non-commissioned officer issued us each a complete set of gear. I remember getting my uniform from the sergeant, who had the rather challenging task of finding pants and shirts from his racks to fit a pencil-thin young woman. When that had been accomplished, the sergeant turned to issue me a pair of black boots.

The black leather made me think the boots were simply men's models like outdoor stores in the Pacific Northwest might have offered at that time. But I had underestimated the Army, which had wonderful boots built on women's lasts. Undoubtedly, the pair of boots I received as an ROTC cadet was the best-fitting footwear I've ever had. As a life-long and compulsive walker, I still have fond memories of those boots, and I've never found their like in the civilian world.

On a Saturday in October, the time came for the freshman ROTC unit to get together and take our first crack at pretending we were soldiers. We ran through the woods on a gorgeous fall day, with sunlight streaming through the trees just starting to lose their golden, red, and orange leaves. In my wonderful boots, dressed in Army pants and a shirt that looked just like my classmates, I got a taste of the strong camaraderie of military life. In a few hours, my fellow students and I went from being a miscellaneous collection of awkward freshmen to a much more solidified social group with a new identity.

While I ran through the woods, trying to respond to the instructions being called out by the ROTC personnel, I was launched onto an internal high, a bit like previous mystical experiences in my life. A gorgeous, sunny Saturday spent in the woods away from my books, the spirit of cooperation with my classmates, intense exercise, and learning about a whole new part of the world may have contributed to my grand feelings. As I ran up a hill covered by dry leaves and threw myself down the draw beyond it, I was finally free of homesickness. My delight then skyrocketed, to the point that it was so astronomical it amazed me. This was better than the sweetest evenings with my high school boyfriends. I didn't know where all the joy had come from, but I drank it in with my whole self.

At age 18, I had no framework for thinking of my experiences in medical terminology. Instead, as I walked back to my dorm on the far side of campus, I turned over in my mind what had happened simply in personal terms. From what I could tell, I had become rapidly, intoxicatingly "high" in the woods due to my sense of belonging with my classmates and the call to service that the Army offered us. Lord knew I was idealistic – that was what had brought me to Princeton. Perhaps what I felt was an inner response to what should be my calling in life. Why not sign up for ROTC – and reap the benefits of a full-ride scholarship as well as ultimately dedicating myself to the ideal of serving my country?

But there was something that troubled me as I walked home. The strong pull I felt toward idealism and service – an impulse the Army seemed ready to help me address – was potentially quite tricky. Running through the woods, wanting to do everything I could for members of my team, being part of a group trying to protect our fellow citizens, all of that made good sense to me. But, at its core, the military was about the threat to coerce and kill people, and the willingness to follow through on those threats.

As I neared my dorm, I quickly but clearly made up my mind that if I ever did have to kill someone, it would not be because I was following orders handed down to me through a top-down authoritative structure like the Army. My understanding of service – and hence morality as I could see it – required something different from me, something that might be fueled by internal idealism but would leave responsibility for my actions squarely on my shoulders. Although I was still wearing the Army uniform when I reached my dorm room, I knew my days in the ROTC class were numbered. I earned my P.E. credit, then turned in my gear at the end of the semester. I was glad for my broadening experience that fall, but equally glad I never signed up for any obligation to the military.

Making new friends, trying on Army clothes for size, and throwing myself into demanding classes were the grand parts of the fall of my freshman year. But as good as such features of my life were, and I valued them all, the nightly pains that had started to plague me in high school were growing rapidly stronger. As the fall progressed, the darkness inside me blossomed. On the one hand, my personal and intellectual life was expanding, and I loved that. On the other hand, I crossed the line from being an uneasy insomniac to suffering from stronger mental illness.

Simply put, the symptoms that had started in my hometown grew exponentially when I hit Princeton's campus. As the fall deepened and November darkness gathered around campus earlier each afternoon, I fell into a new depth of suffering like a cobble down a well. Abruptly, I felt certain that I was nothing less than deeply evil. It seemed suddenly clear that my soul was corrupt, perhaps even responsible for a good measure of the worst in the world around me. That my thinking became so self-centered and negative so quickly is almost more than I can now get my head around. But I dropped headlong into a dark and distorted place where I genuinely felt loathing and contempt for myself, believing at some deep level that I was evil while my friends around me were good.

One consequence of my new framework of thinking was the belief that I didn't merit full portions of food at the cafeteria. Thus, I ate less as the autumn progressed, so I went from being a thin young woman to a painfully scrawny one. Soon I was down to 112 pounds covering my 5 foot 6-inch frame. In the inverted world I had fallen into, feeling hunger pangs was one of my few physical pleasures. When I exercised enough that my muscles and joints ached, I felt doubly good about the suffering I experienced because I deserved it so richly. More weight soon dropped off me, and I could see the contours of all my ribs and of my pelvic bones when I showered.

But remarkably enough, if basics like food didn't seem necessary for my life, the world of ideas still deeply mattered to me. I was a young, bull-headed, determined woman who had crossed the nation to study on the East Coast. My schoolwork came first in my life. It sometimes took every scrap of my self-discipline to pull off, but I concentrated on my daily studies despite my emotional and physical suffering. Again and again, I was rewarded for my efforts to study with explosions in learning, which led me to internal highs I simply loved. While I may not have been eating enough, I was well nourished by my classes.

I also soon had good friends with whom to talk and do things like argue politics. However, I noticed my university friends didn't talk about the kind of peak experiences I had known when I was younger and still living in the Northwest. They were apparently innocent of mystical life, which puzzled me but I simply had to accept. To explore what my earlier experiences might mean, I looked to books. The library at Princeton Theological Seminary, near the university campus, provided me with many volumes on religious experience.

I spent a number of afternoons at a desk in the library's main reference room, avoiding my assigned work in German or philosophy while reading the works of classic Christian mystics. I was comforted to find there were apparently some other souls in the world who had experiences such as what I knew. But my tormented, insomniac states didn't seem to fit with the mystical tradition as it was portrayed in the books I happened to read. Besides that, no mystic I read described experiences in quite the way I would have written about what I had known. Without any further context in which to place my mystical life, I was unsure what to really make of it.

I turned 19 the first winter I was at Princeton. What I knew as a freshman was that while I loved the intellectual life of the university, I was rapidly descending into a hellish state of cruel insomnia and the very deepest alarm. I went to the health service and asked for sleeping pills, but the doctor I saw wouldn't give them to me, explaining they could become habit-forming and that a young person couldn't truly need them. He advised me that I should find a way to get over my homesickness and sleep on my own.

The doctor recommended hot milk before bed, and an R.N. I saw another day at the health service advised me to drink herbal tea. I wanted to explain that such mild remedies were meaningless in my world, and it wasn't simple homesickness causing me problems. But I couldn't find the words to explain that the torment I was living with had started when I was still in high school and that it involved features much deeper than just being away from my family.

Early in the spring semester of my freshman year, desperate for relief from suffering and searching for some sleep, I bought my first bottle of whiskey. Reasonably enough, because all I wanted was the drug effect of the alcohol, I bought the cheapest "rot gut" the liquor store sold. That bottle, in turned out, did help me sleep, at least in one way. If I drank a glass that was the equivalent of six or eight shots and crawled into bed, I felt an explosion of warmth in my stomach. Then, as the alcohol entered my brain, I relaxed and, often enough, fell asleep.

Although I felt terrible in the morning, I repeated the process the next night, for lying in bed awake but in the company of my darkest thoughts was a greater hell than being hung over the next day. It took me a long time to figure out that, over time, alcohol made the demons within me stronger, and it took me still longer to quit drinking. But, in the short run, alcohol helped me cope, at least enough that I stayed enrolled in college and continued to seek the highs I felt while studying during the day.

As soon as I began serious drinking, I felt the necessity of disguising my dependency from others. That was partly the case because I was dedicated to denying what I was doing to myself. I hid my bottles in a dresser drawer and only drank from them when my roommate left the room. Perhaps because I was a Sunday school girl and such a serious university student, it never occurred to my friends that I was a closet lush. But as the spring progressed, I became more set in my ways, drinking significant amounts of the cheapest whiskey most nights.

At the end of my freshman year, I realized that I simply could not continue as a student. I had an impressive transcript of grades, something near a straight-A average. But after a school year of torment and suffering, I had lost a great deal of weight and a good measure of basic physical strength. My friends and family worried about my eating habits, and even I was sometimes appalled to see that so little flesh covered my bones. It also was disorienting for me to find that long walks or other exercise truly tapped what little bodily energy I still had. In short, by the end of that increasingly difficult school year, my roommates, parents, and I all realized I was ill, even if the Princeton health service did not know how to help me.

Although I certainly had no way of diagnosing what was wrong, the only thing I could think to do was to return home and hope life would improve. So, after the end of my first year, I packed up my two hand-me-down suitcases and headed back home.

It's obvious that my life would have turned out quite differently if I didn't have the good fortune of a quick mind, a strong work ethic – and most importantly of all – unquestioning family support. Throughout my early adulthood, my parents were my rock, people on whom I could count to feed and house me when I was deeply ill. Simply put, I owe them my life, not just because they brought me into the world and raised me, but because they gave me a refuge whenever I needed it – and as time would tell, I would need their help again and again. When I came home from Princeton in the summer after my freshman year, they didn't know what was wrong with their beloved daughter. But they were willing to do anything they could to be useful.

I stayed home the following school year, working part-time and taking a couple of classes at the state university next to which I had grown up. Sometime that fall, my mother talked me into seeing a clinical psychologist. That took courage on her part, given the general stigma associated with mental illness, particularly in that era. It also took some strength for me to go, but I did with my parent's support. Those sessions were a good first attempt to address what was clearly wrong with my health, problems so deep my education and life had been fully disrupted.

Quite early in the treatment process, the psychologist diagnosed me as suffering from depression. I accepted that diagnosis with the uncritical approach that comes easily to a 19-year-old. My parents also accepted it because – after all – the psychologist was an authority in such matters.

In fairness to the doctor I saw, I likely didn't volunteer anything about my intense highs and mystical experiences. Equally problematic, if asked about unusual sounds or voices, I'm sure I denied hearing them. I took most seriously the note of warning I had heard from the pediatrician whom I had told about the maniacal laughter, and I lived with thick layers of denial about the auditory symptoms I experienced. So, a diagnosis of simple depression is what the psychologist came up with, and my parents and I accepted that as being what was wrong with me.

In 1979, young people weren't put on medication at anything like the frequency they are today. The psychologist didn't refer me to a psychiatrist who could have prescribed drugs such as lithium, nor did he even discuss the possibility of medication with me. Instead, the psychologist and I worked together on techniques to help me cope with stress and aid me in the battle against insomnia.

We spent our time on progressive muscle relaxation and positive imagery. I wanted it all to work, and I threw myself into the lessons just as I had into my classes at Princeton. When what the psychologist and I practiced didn't seem to make much difference, I assumed it was because I was a poor student of what I was being taught. If only I did the relaxation techniques better, I thought, or perhaps exercised outdoors more, got up earlier, or maybe ate more vegetables, I could get the upper hand on the demons. But try as I might to implement the programs the psychologist gave me, I still remained a victim to my fluctuating and painful internal states.

Still, as that school year away from Princeton progressed, things did improve. I gradually, if partially, recovered. I ate more and developed increasing physical stamina. I put on some much-needed weight, and I slept a bit better. I swam laps, and that seemed to help a smidgen all around. I didn't know why I slowly made progress, but the psychologist encouraged me throughout that school year, saying that depression could be long, but it always came to an end. By spring, my family and I thought I had been through an episode of major depression, but I had come out of it. We hoped what might well be the worst part of my life was in the rearview mirror. Certainly, we all expected I could go forward into a much brighter day.

"I think now you're launched," my mother said as the two of us were packing my things for a return to Princeton for my second year at the university. "You just seem so much more like yourself now."

I concurred. The storm had passed, I thought, and I had great expectations for smoother sailing.

When I look back at that time, I'm glad my family and I didn't know how terrible life would be for me when I was in my 20s and beyond. Sometimes it's good to be protected against knowledge of what you cannot influence. As it turned out, some 35 years passed before I received the full diagnosis of what ailed me. If my parents and I had known the magnitude of what was really wrong, I would likely have never returned to the East. In those days, young people labeled with major mental illness such as schizoaffective disorder were not integrated into college life to the degree students are now. It might have been the end of my education if I had had a full and correct diagnosis when I first met with a psychologist at age 19. Because I value my schooling so highly, I am glad I got it when I was young and it was available to me.

But, of course, I wouldn't choose that anyone else be misdiagnosed or ineffectively treated for major mental illness. For one thing, there's a real and ongoing risk of suicide. As time would tell, it was simple chance that I avoided that kind of death during my Ivy League education. Still, I so deeply value the life of the mind I can only be glad I didn't know at age 19 that I was a person with a grave illness. Simply put, I relished my years as a student even when I was within spitting distance of death. Maybe only a crazy person can appreciate such a perspective. But the dice of my life were being rolled when I returned to Princeton, and in my case, I'm glad I dared to let them bounce in the direction of an amazing education – no matter the cost to my physical and emotional health. We each have only one life to risk for what we value, and I think it's a privilege to clearly place our ultimate bets on what we deeply cherish, including the simple but vital love of learning.

CHAPTER 2:

RETURN TO PRINCETON

My second year in college was the one and only interval of adulthood during which my psychiatric symptoms were mostly absent. It was a glorious year, the sweetest, brightest, and best of my life. When I arrived at the university in early September, my friends at Princeton welcomed me back. I was no longer homesick for the Northwest, and I started to feel much more at ease in the East as the hardwood trees turned a fiery orange in October.

To be sure, I did walk a lot to burn off energy, sometimes down to the end of the lake near the university campus and back. That stroll was about 8 miles, roundtrip, from my dorm. As time passed, I walked long distances in great loops through Princeton township. Because I was young and strong, I could keep up a brisk pace no matter how far I went, and I often enough gave myself blisters.

The greatest upside of my energy surges is that physical pain is just a pesky detail. So, time and time again throughout my adult life, my walks have given me major blisters on both feet, often enough with toenails so bruised they later slough off. When the energy lifts me out of myself and I'm really cranking, I walk until my blisters break and my socks are bloody. There's no significant pain involved, just a squishiness inside my shoes I don't find disagreeable. Not everyone, I like to think, can come so close to literally walking their feet off.

I finished up some of my walks in Princeton after dark, which surely wasn't wise. But I didn't consider the matter, and in any event the exercise didn't feel optional. From time to time, I thought it odd that other people at Princeton didn't hoof it all over creation. But perhaps because I'd grown up hiking with my family in the summers, I could often convince myself my behavior was somehow normal.

In a rare financial splurge, I bought a bicycle shortly after returning to campus. It was a simple 3-speed, but I loved to ride it. When the weather was fair, I rode it to class and on short jaunts to places like Princeton's Revolutionary War battlefield. On weekends I took it for much longer spins, leaving Princeton behind and pedaling through the country to the Delaware River. Only once did I persuade a friend to come with me on such a mega-trip, in general, my friends couldn't see a reason to leave their sedentary lives behind. But even just going by myself was fun. I enjoyed the fresh air and change of scenery, as well as the hard physical exercise required to get that tank of a bike up long hills.

My main love was always in the intellectual life fostered at the university. I took everything from calculus to history in the fall when I returned to Princeton. I excelled in philosophy, the subject in which I intended to major. The only class I didn't love was German, but I plowed diligently through my final semester. To this day I have nightmares that, somehow, I really didn't complete the German requirement. In my dreams, I have to return to Princeton and take the final German exam. I walk across the campus to the exam, knowing I am unprepared for it and will fail the test. But, in reality, I took the German exams and scored well enough.

My social life was rich. Despite my year away, I retained several friends from my dorm, students I had known or roomed with my freshman year. Added to that group were some new friends. The dorm in which we lived was called Princeton Inn. It was a large, converted hotel. A long wing led away from the dining hall and common rooms. Separate from those areas was a smaller and darker building that had once housed servants who worked in the hotel. In between that building and the main inn, the university had added some rooms in what was known as "the Addition."

In my freshman year I had lived with two other women in a room at the very end of the hotel's main wing. In my sophomore year I was able to have a single room in the Addition section of the dorm. It was a tiny room, and cold all winter long, but it was helpful to me to have a room all to myself. In particular, when it came time to sleep, I appreciated the fact that no roommates went in or out, or turned on the lights after I had gone to bed.

My life revolved around my studies. But for me one of the most interesting parts of the day was the supper hour. After collecting a tray of food, my friends and I sat at a large table and shot the breeze. The people gathered around that simple table were quite a community. Our evening bull sessions ran the gamut from politics to personal life to what we were studying in our classes. The quality of the conversation was generally high enough I learned a lot simply by taking my evening meal.

It's fair to say that most of my friends were nerds like me, students who took their studies seriously. We typically maintained high grade points in difficult subjects. Even my friends who did not do well overall excelled in some subjects. One example was a sharp young man who earned either A's or F's in his coursework: the former in classes he valued, the latter in classes he didn't like and wholly neglected.

Another friend did such excellent work in the humanities he was what Princeton termed a "university scholar." I knew his intellectual abilities were much above mine, but I was happy to drink in what I could of his thinking during our long supper conversations. As a group, my friends took the life of the mind seriously, often reading books not required by our classwork. In that sense, my idealism had found a strong and natural home within one of Princeton's subcultures.

To be sure, undergraduate life at Princeton contained other subcultures with which I was never at ease. In my day, the grandchildren of the Rockefellers and a few other American dynasties attended Princeton. They appeared to me to live quite different lives from me and my kind. They didn't put in time at work-study jobs during the school year as I did, nor labor during the summers doing things like painting houses as I did back home in Pullman. There was no doubt in my mind they were much more sophisticated and better traveled than me. From my perspective, they kept to themselves – although it's perhaps possible they felt the same way about my friends and me.

My dorm was located at one edge of the university campus, beyond the railroad tracks from other university buildings. Most Princeton undergraduates joined the private eating clubs that lined one street on the far side of campus from where I lived. By choosing to live where we did and not join the clubs, my friends and I put ourselves in the minority. It was likely no accident that many students in racial minority groups also lived in my dorm and didn't join the clubs. In some ways one might say we were social outcasts from the mainline Ivy students. But at least as I experienced our lives, my friends and I had one another to socialize with – and we shared a passion for intellectual life that was not obviously reflected in many of the students who based their social lives on the private eating clubs. Thus, I didn't feel like an outcast but a member of the in-group that I truly valued.

A young man from New York impressed me deeply. He appeared in my life suddenly when he introduced himself to me in the dorm. We joyfully flirted with one another without ever establishing a full-blown relationship. His friends soon became friends of mine, so my social circle in the dorm grew. It was also during my sophomore year that I got to know a faculty wife who served as the "house mother" for the dorm. And I became much better acquainted with a faculty family that came once a week for suppers in our dining hall.

In the spring of my sophomore year, I signed up for a freshman geology class covering Earth history to satisfy part of Princeton's science requirement. As the semester proceeded, I became increasingly intrigued by the lectures, readings, labs and field trips that constituted the course. Like many students of my generation, I had spent much time studying European history. I was deeply impressed that geologists talked about history measured in billions of years rather than in mere centuries. And geology, I learned, could explain everything from the fossil record to the growth of the mountain ranges I loved so much in the West. My classmates and I were taught the clear evidence there was not one Ice Age, but several such bitter intervals, each separated from the others by time so "deep" it is almost unfathomable.

The part of the course that most fascinated me was the evidence that the history of life on Earth was intertwined with the evolution of the physical planet itself. Starting in earliest times billions of years ago, simple organisms in the seas spent their days performing photosynthesis. Those humble life-forms were responsible for the buildup of oxygen in the atmosphere on which we animals now depend. The air itself, I came to understand, reflected the whole history of life on Earth.

In another example of how interconnected life and the physical planet are, I learned how the gradual dispersal of the continents in geologically recent times allowed land-dwelling species of plants and animals to diverge from one another. Then again, life forms like giant ferns living in ancient swamps gave us the carbon-rich deposits we know as coal beds. The fossil fuels that powered the industrial revolution and kept industry humming throughout the 20th century, I understood, were the results of life's long history on the planet.

Best of all, the course was not based on recounting facts we students were expected to accept, digest and regurgitate. The great thing about geology, it seemed to me, was that tangible evidence could be produced for each of its claims. Looking at fossils of earlier life forms, or turning over in my hand rocks formed in ancient seas, all had an immediacy I found delightful. Again and again, as the semester proceeded, I was struck by how much geology could explain and the clear methods the science used to make its claims about the world.

By spring, I was thinking about the geology class almost as much as all my others combined. Far from being merely a course I had to take to fulfill the science requirement, I had come to view introductory Earth history as a gem among all the gems I had found exploring Princeton's course catalog. So, although it was very late in my college career to become a science major, I talked with the faculty member in the geology department who advised undergraduates. At first, he was skeptical that a philosophy student could succeed in his department. But when he learned how high my grades were, he said I could indeed major in geology, if that's what I wanted.

To be sure, there were some real hurdles involved in the possible switch. It was true that I had a good start on college-level math, but I hadn't taken any chemistry or physics. Without chemistry, I couldn't take mineralogy, the junior-level geology class I'd need to jump into come the fall. Even taking the first semester of freshman chemistry during the summer at home, I would still be a semester behind. Beyond that, I'd have to work hard for the remainder of my time in college to pack in all the science and math I'd need to graduate with a first-rate degree – the only kind for which I thought it worth aiming. But despite these challenging issues, I changed my major to geology in the spring of my sophomore year.

The following fall I started to learn what my decision to major in science actually meant, in particular in the junior-level mineralogy course required of all geology majors. I readily enough learned the basics of how scientists described minerals, but there surely did seem to be a lot of the blasted things I was supposed to be able to instantly identify. Then, around mid-semester, the material in the course made a quantum leap upward in difficulty when we started to study how light behaves within crystals. Light does some counter-intuitive things inside minerals, but what happens to the light rays was one of the first ways early geologists with simple lab equipment learned to identify chemical variations in minerals.

In lecture and lab, as we studied the interaction of light and crystals, I was sometimes rather lost, not something that I had had much experience with in school. However, I responded to my initial inability to understand optical mineralogy by redoubling my efforts. For that extra measure of work, I was sometimes rewarded by flashes of understanding that were not profound by any objective measure. However, they were nothing less than intoxicating to me because they were such a pleasure to experience.

In a couple of instances, while studying intensely, I flew up into a blinding flash of joy as I understood another aspect of how light waves behave in complex crystals. Given the rewards of my internal experiences, it was no surprise I bore down in mineralogy and studied more and more. At the end of the semester, I earned an A+ in a difficult course that several of my classmates flunked. Although my professor praised my work on the final exam, my performance was really no credit to me – anyone would have ceaselessly studied in exchange for the episodes of joy that suddenly and swiftly lifted me upward like a rocket.

During that fall long ago, when studying the optics of mineral crystals accelerated my mind into joy, I couldn't know how close I was to renewed internal trouble and grief. As winter dissolved into spring that year, I rapidly slipped into the patterns of distress I had known as a freshman. I couldn't sleep, even after a long day of schoolwork punctuated by a session of swimming laps or walking many miles. Soon enough, everything about my life felt difficult and desperate. My self-contempt returned, quickly reaching high levels. Classes had never seemed so stressful. I had a heavy load of courses as a junior who had switched into the sciences very late, that was true. But I also knew the real trouble wasn't my demanding schedule.

Something was seriously wrong. In addition to wretched levels of insomnia, I soon had ferocious headaches. I returned time and time again to the university health service, but, just as when I was a freshman, the doctors I saw there didn't help me with the physical distress, let alone recognize the psychiatric issue that lay behind them. Discouraged, I could only return to class and try my best to hold my life together.

This period included my first experiences of a particular mental abnormality that's still with me all these decades later. I began to think that rattlesnakes were on the floor near my feet. I knew there were no rattlers in New Jersey, of course, but my childhood memories of them in the inland Northwest were clear and strong. In my distress, I started to think the snakes were coiled on the floor around me, ready to strike at my legs.

When I was sitting, all I could do to protect myself from these phantom-like rattlesnakes was pull my feet up and sit cross legged on my chair. When I was standing and the snakes appeared around me, there really was nothing I could do except move and keep moving, trying to stay a step ahead of the rattlers following behind me and matching my pace. At night the snakes sometimes covered the floor around my bed, in which case all I could do was be careful to keep my arms and legs near the center of the mattress, away from the edges where the mental rattlesnakes might be able to strike at my limbs.

Perhaps it's no surprise that soon I returned to the heavy drinking I'd done in the spring of my freshman year. A couple of my geology classmates were good at hitting the bottle, so this time, I had company in pursuing oblivion by way of ethanol. We didn't drink to enjoy an unusual brand of ale, let alone savor some fine wine. We drank hard liquor intending to get drunk – a goal we always achieved, usually rapidly.

During this period, I first drank to the point of blacking out. I could have been alarmed about what I had done when I sobered up, but instead I simply adapted to my new normal. To rationalize my behavior, I could compare what I was doing to the similar exploits of a few friends around me – never mind that most of my classmates didn't voluntarily kill their brain cells by pickling them in alcohol to the point they didn't know how a particular night had ended.

Still, in fairness to my young self, it was a bit difficult in undergraduate life to see where fairly common drinking levels stopped and problem behavior began. A great deal of student social life at Princeton was – and still is – fueled by alcohol, including the excessive consumption of it. Parties focused on alcohol, complete with competitive drinking games, ran at Princeton from Thursday evening through early Sunday morning. And alcohol abuse at Princeton doesn't end with student life. The university's main event for alumni, a campus-wide bash held just before commencement each June, is celebrated with plenty of school spirit and bottled spirits.

In some ways, at least, I fit in with college life better when I was drinking compulsively than when I abstained from alcohol altogether. Perhaps, I was plagued by increasingly painful internal states during the spring semester, fitting in with the undergraduate milieu had strong appeal, even beyond what most young people feel tugging at them in that direction. Beyond that, the reward of drinking, at least on the time scale of a few hours, was a substantial release from psychic pain. True, hangovers in the morning were unmitigated hell, and in the midst of them I often vowed to stay clear of the bottle forever. But I went back to drinking time and time again for the sake of release and the promise of sleep, if only in a blacked-out stupor.

Nevertheless, even though I was drinking myself into unconsciousness, I was still a serious student. I always made it to class and lab and finished my work. At the end of spring semester, to celebrate the conclusion of our last final exam, two good friends who were also majoring in geology gathered in my room. We each brought a bottle of hard liquor to the event. Eric, who could more than keep up with me in alcohol abuse, drank, talked, shouted and sang until the small morning hours, but ultimately made it back to his room for the night. Andy, a brilliant student but a novice in the world of drinking, collapsed on my floor after Eric left. I threw a coat over him, then crawled onto my bed fully dressed, content I had on the one hand kept up all night with the hardest drinker I knew – and on the other hand I had easily drunk more than the smartest kid in our class. Such, at the time, were my peculiar standards for success.

One aspect of the quest to become an adult would shape my life for years to come. For some reason, when I was an undergraduate, I believed earning a Ph.D. was a requirement for adult life. I'm not sure why, but a doctorate seemed a fundamental requirement of growing up, a bit like getting a driver's license, having sex, or voting for President. Of course, my father had a Ph.D., and that meant I was familiar with the general plan of going on for graduate work. But my father never pressured me to go on for a doctorate. When I think about it, I realize that most people don't think that graduate degrees are to be expected of all the souls who inhabit this troubled world, but then I'm peculiar – and I have the psychiatric record to prove it.

During my junior year in college, it became clear that to earn a doctoral degree in the geological sciences from a prestigious university, I needed a broader and deeper training in math and physical sciences than I could reasonably get in my senior year. To put it another way, it mattered that I was an ex-philosophy major. My transcript read like I was a late convert to empirical studies, and that wouldn't put me in a good position to get admitted to the type of graduate program I valued. From what I could tell, I either needed to earn a master's degree in geology – likely at a large university in the West – or else somehow supplement my undergraduate coursework with further studies. I couldn't simply stay at Princeton for a fifth year – it wasn't permitted. But I could take a year off, just as I had done after my freshman year.

I talked to my parents about my situation. I knew they valued helping me with my educational goals, so I emphasized that my studies in geology at Princeton were going well. Still, my undergraduate career would essentially end before I was ready to start a doctorate at another Ivy university. They accepted my word about that, and I didn't mislead them. But what I didn't tell them, I'm sad now to say, is that the hellish state of my mind at the end of my junior year really compelled me to leave Princeton for a second year off. I simply couldn't sleep enough – even with heavy drinking – to function at the intellectual level I wanted.

In the spring of my junior year, I knew I needed to change something significant to get some sleep, ease up on the booze, and somehow get away from at least the most vivid and persistent experiences of rattlesnakes. But unlike how I felt about matters at the end of my freshman year, I didn't want to return to my small hometown situated in the middle of wheat fields. Instead, I wanted to head to Seattle, where I thought I'd feel more like the adult I was, in fact, becoming. I explained to my parents that I could work as a lab tech at the University of Washington, and take classes like differential equations and freshman physics on the side. My deeply generous parents agreed to help me with the transition. Their financial and emotional support, as always, was on tap for my needs.

While I wish I had been able to tell my parents more about what ailed me, I also don't think my behavior was unusual. Young people tormented by mental illness often cannot articulate what's wrong – just as their families can sometimes not see how to be useful beyond simply being as supportive as possible.

But before I could start my year at the University of Washington, I needed to go to a summer course called Field Camp, in which all geology students enroll. My Princeton classmates were joined by students from other universities, going through a six-week camp headquartered outside Red Lodge, Montana. The class taught us the basics of making geological maps and interpreting rocks, faults, fossils, and topography. The course alternated between rather demanding geological work and easier events like a visit to Yellowstone. One day we stood on warm ground near an underground coal fire, on another day we looked at fossils imbedded by the millions in rocks, and on another we bathed in hot springs.

When one young man offered to share his chewing tobacco with me, I learned the pleasure of bigger jolts of nicotine than anything I'd known from cigarettes. Another friend gave me several cigars and I was glad to adopt them as a summertime habit. If you have never had a wad of chewing tobacco in your cheek while you smoked a big stogie, you don't know what nicotine can really do for the brain. I enjoyed both the rush of the stimulant, and also the comforting ritual of smoking. As I liked to say back then, if I didn't get cancer, it wasn't going to be my fault.

My relationship with alcohol was built on a deep ambivalence, resting as it did on the full knowledge that the staggering pain of a terrible hangover would follow the blissful release of each drunken stupor. My relationship with tobacco was much purer – I loved it without reservation. Considering that I often suffered acutely from the effects of insomnia and high-energy states, I don't understand why a stimulant swept me off my feet. But treasure nicotine, I surely did.

Chewing tobacco packed such a wallop in my skinny little body, I felt I could run a 4-minute mile. The fact that I was the only woman I knew who put a wad of tobacco in her cheek added to my pleasure in taking big doses of nicotine on board. To slow down a bit, I could get a smaller fix by smoking, usually cigarettes, but occasionally cigars or, briefly, a corn-cob pipe. I actually liked the smell of tobacco smoke, and I deeply appreciated the simple ceremony of sharing a light with another smoker. Such moments, I still think of as a kind of secular Eucharist. The fact that smokers were beginning to be condemned as sinners when I was young also had its charm, and I found I deeply appreciated the company of smokers I met through the initial sharing of a match.

To be sure, there were times I quit all nicotine delivery devices. Indeed, I went on the wagon several times in both college and graduate school. I knew the stimulation of nicotine, especially on top of my coffee habit, was the last thing I needed. As I lay in bed at night, tossing and turning with insomnia, I would vow to quit, or at least quit earlier in the day. Eventually I consciously came to realize that nicotine could make my mental rattlesnakes stronger. That surely gave me good grounds to stop, but nicotine is a tough habit to break – even more so than alcohol, many would say. I quit smoking and chewing several times over the years, staying away from both for considerable periods. But tobacco had a strong undercurrent for me, one that pulled me back to it more times than I can now recollect.

But strongly unusual events in my head continued during Field Camp. At dawn one morning in Yellowstone, I awoke in my sleeping bag and was plunged into an experience the like of which I'd not known before. Suddenly there seemed to be searing sunlight hitting my brain all around my skull. The scorching light didn't come from my eyes, but bathed my brain from every direction inside my head. Alarmed, I struggled upright. Because I didn't care to wake my sleeping classmates and announce I was going insane, I simply sat on my sleeping bag with my head between my knees. When the experience ended a few minutes later, I collapsed as I had been. I was exhausted, hung over, and I'd just been through the most alarming experience of my life. The terrible trip, which has happened a couple of times since that morning, is what I called "dawn screaming hell" for when it first overtook me. I would not wish it on my worst enemy.

I was deeply confused by what had happened that memorable dawn. I turned the experience over in my mind. Was it just drinking a great deal was catching up to me? I couldn't say, but I knew that alcohol wasn't going to make things easier in the long run.

With work, my classmates and I got through Field Camp. My geology friends were to return to Princeton in September, I stopped at home, then went on to Seattle. The terrible feelings I had been living with gradually eased as I adjusted to classes and work at the University of Washington. I was helped that fall because I loved a math class I took. I have no real talent for mathematics, being only able to solve problems like an engineer, not draw up proofs or truly speak the language of math. But I was delighted to find in a class on differential equations that I could calculate things like the trajectory of an Apollo re-entry capsule returning to Earth, a situation in which the force of gravity is both pulling at an object and changing in strength as the object moves over time.

I sat at a red Formica table, studying my maroon differential equations textbook for hours on end. Perhaps it helped that, for a change, my math instructor was a woman who neatly laid out solutions to exercises on the blackboard at the front of the classroom. While it may sound strange to think a person's emotional life can be helped by studying math, exactly that was true for me that fall. The intensity of the experience of learning made me high, and, for a change, the high was relatively measured and didn't lead to darkness at night.

A friend I made in math class volunteered her viewpoint of me one day when we were finishing up a study session. "You're a real student," she said with admiration. "I've never known the like of you."

While I was flattered by that observation, I also wasn't entirely sure it was true. A real student, I imagined, would study out of purely positive motivations. As I knew from the inside of my confused life, I was at least partly motivated to concentrate on abstract topics because they were an escape from the rattlesnakes and the other pains of my daily existence.

On quite a different front, I made a significant change during my year in Seattle. Rather irrationally, I hoped it would lessen the pain woven into my life. The change concerned my name. I had been named Elsa Kirsten Peterson at birth and always called Elsa. My name, to state the obvious, was Scandinavian.

Confused as I was by returning waves of internal suffering, I latched onto the idea that if I were less Scandinavian, I could be less unwell. It seemed to me that Europe's most northern people were a seriously depressed group, and I had been taught to call my mental problems "depression." Many of the films of Ingmar Bergman I'd seen at Princeton were sharp downers, as were many of the writings of Per Lagerkvist and other Scandinavian authors I had read.

If I were divorced from my father's Swedish roots, I came to hope, I'd have a better chance of being well. I therefore decided to morph my name toward what I hoped might at least bring me better luck, going by my middle name rather than my first and modifying Peterson to become Peters. I didn't make the change to distance myself from my family, whom I loved deeply. But I desperately wanted to do anything I could to tame the torment of my mind.

Thus, I started to go by E. Kirsten Peters, a name I hoped might pass for British or simply thoroughly American rather than Scandinavian.

Looking back at it, my decision to modify my name rested on my inner admission, reached for the first time, that I was deeply and chronically ill. It wasn't that I'd suffered from one, isolated wave of what the doctor called depression during my freshman year, as my family and I had been hoping. My suffering had returned with a vengeance, and when it did so at least one part of me knew I was truly and fundamentally unwell.

Obviously, changing my name didn't help matters – but neither had the relaxation techniques the psychologist at home taught me. So, I tried to escape my chronic suffering as best I could. Without effective help from the doctors, the best idea I could come up with was to modify my birth name.

Although a different name could not cure me, my brain and body were functioning much better by the onset of the soggy winter of my year in Seattle than when I had staggered away from Princeton. I was drinking only sporadically and, in time, I tapered off entirely. As a mild spring moved over Seattle, I healed still more slowly. By June, I was feeling pretty well.

My personal life in Seattle grew much more complex due to a casual fling I had with a lithe Middle Eastern young man who lived in the same building where I rented a studio apartment. After a few weeks of involvement with him, I realized I was overdue to menstruate. The situation was deeply alarming because I was an extremely regular woman who could all but set her watch to the moment her next menstrual period would start. Missing my period was unheard of for me, and I deeply dreaded what it could mean.

Back then, no pregnancy tests were available in drug stores. I waffled about going to the health service to inquire about my condition. I was embarrassed by, as well as afraid of, my situation. Potentially becoming a mother owing to a brief association with a man from outside my orbit seemed the most asinine situation I could have dreamed up for myself. I talked to a divorced woman friend from my math class about the situation. She sympathized and encouraged me to have patience.

"Your body may still make it clear you're not pregnant," she advised.

After another couple of weeks, I found myself in my tiny bathroom doubled over with cramps and bleeding profusely. Never had I welcomed a menstrual period with such joy. In the end, strongly sobered by the whole experience, I vowed to do much better about contraception.

I was on firmer ground in intellectual and professional life than in my thoughtless sexual life. While in Seattle I had kept in touch with the faculty member at Princeton who had taught the class in optical mineralogy I had enjoyed so much, the one that led to intoxicating mystical experiences I still treasure. Corresponding with Prof. Lincoln

Hollister, I asked if there were any chance I could work in his lab in the summer before my senior year at Princeton. Luckily, he had grant support available. I therefore headed back to Princeton to work for Lincoln in June.

The summer's work was intense, but it was also a pleasure. Each day I labored with a complex instrument that filled a small room in the cool basement of the geology building. My efforts over the summer were to be the core of my senior thesis research. I started my senior year in the fall in good shape regarding my thesis research.

But it was also true my Princeton friends had gone on without me, graduating and starting their working lives or going to graduate school. My struggle with illness, quite clearly, had cost me. Although I still tried to deny I was different from the people around me in some ways, my two years away from Princeton meant I was to be a college student for six years, rather than the usual four. Walking through Princeton's familiar campus, but without the friends and classmates I had known, made me feel acutely lonely. What I had to do was to launch myself into a new round of work and make new friends as I began my final year at the university.

Senior year went well for me. In earlier semesters I had fulfilled my "work study" obligations by working about 10 hours a week at the circulation desk of the main library. But throughout my senior year I worked in Lincoln's lab, which propelled my senior thesis work forward and paid me the minimum wage. Glad for the job for several different reasons, I threw myself into the work of making chemical analyses of minerals at a microscopic scale. The work rested on an electron microscope, a device that beamed energy onto smoothly polished minerals at a microscopic level. I loved the challenge of the work and was soon producing a mountain of data, a fine step forward toward the large project known as my senior thesis.

But my mental peculiarities held back one part of my academic work. In the fall of my senior year, I took a graduate class from Lincoln Hollister, the same faculty member from whom I had earlier taken the undergraduate mineralogy class that had often blinded me with joy. The graduate course was quite a different experience. I've always had trouble with intense day-dreams, and sitting through Lincoln's lectures on metamorphic rocks I frequently spaced out. It wasn't that I found the lectures boring – far from it. It was just that I wasn't able to concentrate on them for long.

Again and again, I would find myself at the end of the lecture hour with just a couple lines of notes and no memory of what had been discussed. My involuntary day-dreams regularly sabotaged my best efforts to be studious that fall. In graduate courses, at least as they are taught in the Ivy League, there are no textbooks. That meant the material I missed in lecture owing to my daydreams was impossible to find elsewhere. As I experienced them, the lectures became nightmarish episodes of paying attention for a little while, only to again find I had lost track of everything for most of the hour. I had had similar problems in other classes earlier in life, but Lincoln's graduate course moved so quickly through such abstract material I was extremely dazed and confused when I woke up to my surroundings at the end of each class.

I soldiered on, doing my best, trying to learn all I could from my fellow students in lab sessions. But there was no question I was handicapped in my efforts. Ultimately, I settled with relief for a B grade rather than my more common A mark. It wasn't the end of the world, but it did alert me to yet another way my mind apparently worked compared to the more numerous normal people around me. And that, I'm sure, made me feel alone once more with my inner experiences.

Still, as the fall of my senior year deepened, I began to feel more at home at Princeton than I ever had in the past. There were still some mental rattlesnakes on the floor to be sure, but I could often truly feel life was good and I was firmly embedded in a fine institution. For anyone who loves to study – either due to the love of learning itself or due to internal highs experienced while hitting the books – one's college years are fundamentally a pleasure.

Soon I made new friends to help replace those who had graduated without me. At least as I experienced it, Princeton had rich and diverse subcultures within its student body. Although I continued to avoid the private eating clubs associated with the university, I was fortunate to fall into friendships with undergraduates at the dining hall where I ate and with graduate students in the geology department with whom I spent time in the labs. Once again, as during my sophomore year, I felt the warm bonds of intense, youthful friendship sustaining me day-by-day. If anything helps a person in the struggle to live with major mental illness, I suspect it's a feeling of belonging. I've been fortunate to fall into various communities during my life, and I've always been grateful for that fact.

During my senior year I got to know my advisor much better. His dark hair had the hint of a wave in it, and perhaps the odd gray hair. He had glasses he used for reading and for looking at minerals and rocks. He led an adventuresome life, doing geology in the wilderness of the mountains of western Canada. Later, after I had left Princeton, he moved his field studies to the Himalayas. Although he was much better traveled than I was, we had a love of the outdoors, as well as a love for minerals, in common.

I deeply valued seeing a research scientist in his daily life, and my relationship with Lincoln gave me my first clear taste of what my own working life might be like someday. At some point, I came up with the idea of reading all of Lincoln's professional publications. Doing so, I thought, could give me a way of looking at a scientist's life-long professional output. Because Lincoln's work was varied – ranging from the study of mountain-building processes in British Columbia to the analysis of moon rocks brought back to Earth by the Apollo missions – the reading was both interesting and truly educational. It marked another step forward in my intellectual life, teaching me what a person's scientific output could be like over time.

Another faculty connection I made during my senior year was with the Geology Department's chairman. Sheldon Judson was nearing retirement, with thin, graying hair and eyes a bit magnified behind thick glasses. But although he was old, Sheldon was still actively involved in the life of the university, including taking a special interest in us undergraduates. Although I didn't know Sheldon well, I found his gentle grace and humor a delightful addition to my life in the geology department. As it turned out, in later years my friendship with Sheldon would blossom to such an extent that I count getting to know him a bit as one of the most significant experiences of my senior year.

Then, there was a sexual relationship I won't forget. I hooked up with a pleasant, gentle young man from Chinatown in New York City. Soon Junjie and I were spending our evenings together. The physical aspect of the relationship was exceedingly pleasant, and Junjie's agreeable personality meant our association was easy to sustain. But as the winter of that year unfolded it became clear Junjie was seriously procrastinating about his senior thesis work. All Princeton students are required to write a senior thesis, and virtually all seniors produce a document that can be given at least a passing grade. Given my compulsion to work hard and generate whatever the university required of me, Junjie's failure to even start writing his thesis in East Asian Studies was inexplicable. I tried to be supportive and encouraging, but I was increasingly mystified about what my friend was doing to himself. As the winter faded into spring and Junjie still had not properly begun his work, I started to feel fully overwhelmed by the situation.

To me, school work was a life-line, a way of combatting the illness I was so often engulfed in. To see a person choose not to do his school work was deeply frightening. If I ever journeyed down the road of procrastination, I realized I would lose hold of what literally helped me survive my problems. Perhaps, given the contours of my life, I simply couldn't respond well to a procrastinator, no matter his other virtues and despite our close relationship.

Looking back at the spring of my senior year I've always felt guilt that I didn't somehow do more to help Junjie. But in addition to my fear of what my friend was choosing, I suppose I was also caught up in my own work and plans. As always, I was primarily focused on doing the best possible work I could in my academic pursuits. I also was in the midst of applying to elite graduate programs in geology. In the end, I withdrew from Junjie emotionally, put my head down, and finished all my work with my usual intensity. Junjie completed his classes but didn't write his thesis and thus could not graduate.

I wish with my whole heart I had had the wit and wisdom to better help my friend. I'm sure my distancing of myself from Junjie was an added blow to him, and I regret that deeply. But as a young woman who was flooded with her own powerful fears of failure, all I could do as I saw my friend academically drowning was save myself. The decision to withdraw from Jungie, a turning point that was much more instinctive than conscious, is one I hope I would not have so blindly chosen in later, more mature, years. But, as a senior in college, I allowed my instincts to determine my actions and I put distance between myself and a good and gentle man just when he needed everyone's help.

Other events in the spring of that year conspired to pull me forward. I had applied to graduate school at Harvard, Yale, Penn State and the University of Michigan. I was admitted to all four programs. I had also applied for a fellowship from the National Science Foundation, and I was delighted when I was notified that I would receive the three-year award. After quick trips to Penn State and Harvard, I followed my brother's advice and enrolled at the latter institution.

The geology department there had its complexities, but as Nils put it, a doctorate from Harvard could help open doors to whatever might come up later in my life. Thus, I packed for graduation and began to take my leave of my alma mater. My early youth was coming to a close. Although I would remain a student for six more years, the day I graduated from college felt like a significant turning point, one that propelled me into financial independence from my parents and established me as an adult in the world.

My parents and my brother came to New Jersey for commencement. I was able to introduce them to Lincoln and his wife Sarah, and to Sheldon. It was a wonderful time, a true celebration of what I'd accomplished as a student and of the best values of the institution I had grown to deeply love. Still, despite all the reasons I had to be happy –

and I was all but wrapped in joy at graduation – I also knew the rattlesnakes of my mind were not far off. As time would tell, the snakes would not only swarm on the floor around me at Harvard, they would take me to deeper depths than I had ever known, including to a state that threatened my life.

CHAPTER 3:

HARVARD YEARS

Although I was continuing my education in geology, my academic role when I entered Harvard changed significantly. As a college student at Princeton, I had taken classes in a wide range of subjects. Philosophy, history, German, chemistry, math, and religion classes filled my dance card and merited my attention. As a Ph.D. student, I took almost exclusively geology classes, mostly from just two faculty members in my department.

It was understood by all concerned that one of those two professors would be my advisor, a role of the utmost importance in the life of a Ph.D. student in the sciences. Graduate education is a system of training that's strongly modeled on the tradition that goes back to the medieval roots of European universities. And particularly in the sciences, graduate training replicates the master-apprentice relationship, with intensive laboratory work substituting for labor in the workshops of old.

In addition to my new role within academic culture, there was another transition to make. I found that the atmosphere of my new university was quite unlike my previous one, at least as I experienced it. Harvard is a fine university, but it's quite an odd place in one respect. Many people at all levels of the institution invest time and energy telling themselves – and anyone else who will listen – that Harvard is the best, the finest, the greatest university in the nation and, indeed, in the world.

That claim is, of course, absurd. In a given area of research, MIT or Stanford may be undisputed national leaders. In another arena, Cornell or Berkeley may have the strongest programs. Although it may astound people embedded in the Eastern establishment, in many applied subjects, the sprawling land-grant universities outside New England are the key players in both research and teaching. Nevertheless, the name

Harvard does loom large, and a number of people at the institution, particularly the faculty, seem to suffer from the need to chronically posture and preen, assuring themselves that because they are associated with the university, they are the world's leaders in their field. This self-congratulatory atmosphere was a strange backdrop to what I hoped would be an engaging education in my field.

But I didn't have much time to critique the atmosphere of my new home. Soon I was involved in the whirlwind studies of an intensive doctoral program. I lived in a drab, graduate dormitory just across the street from the two buildings that housed my department, and I ate many meals in the law school cafeteria on the other side of my dorm. My first year of Harvard life was largely defined by those four buildings, each only yards from the others. I attended classes, studied, ate hurried meals, then repeated the cycle. My life may have been quite narrow and monastic, but it was also enormously interesting.

At Harvard I was soon digging much deeper into my branch of natural science than ever before, which led me to sustained intellectual highs. Intense study likely only appeals to idealists, people motivated more by ideas than the practical parts of life. I had always been such a person who would trade away her supper for a good book. In that sense, graduate work was designed for me and I reveled in it. Pouring ideas into my head, day and night, was a joy, one familiar from my time at Princeton, but now more focused.

But my life was not entirely defined by study. My habit of burning off excess energy by walking for miles continued from my earlier days. I generally didn't know exactly where I was when I walked during my first year as a graduate student, but it didn't much matter. If I walked from Harvard down through the housing projects to the neighborhood of MIT and crossed a bridge, I was in Boston. To get home, I would simply reverse my steps. If I walked in another direction, I would go deep into the heart of Somerville. I could walk up the Charles River as a change from the previous two journeys. For a shorter walk, I would stride to a reservoir that lay in Cambridge itself, circle it, and come back to campus.

I knew my habit of long walks, and most especially the compulsive ones that occurred at night, could get me into trouble at any time. Cambridge – unlike Princeton – has a significant crime rate. I took a risk each time I walked by myself for miles and miles, in particular after dark. Due to those risks, I did try on at least two occasions to rein in my energy by swimming laps in a university pool rather than walking. I had been a regular lap swimmer at Princeton, where the pool hours and the pool location had suited my life. But at Harvard, the hours the pool was open didn't seem to match my schedule and the big pool lay rather inconveniently down through campus and then across the Charles River. So, despite the risks, I walked a great deal my first year in graduate school.

Later in my time in Cambridge I was to gain greatly from one particular effect of my walks. Because I traversed so many of the streets and lanes of the city, it was inevitable that, simply by chance, I would at some point walk through Longfellow Park. My steps took me in front of a small brick building with an equally small sign in front of it announcing it was "Friends Meeting at Cambridge." The first time I went by the Meetinghouse I simply kept walking.

As with all of my travels on foot, I wasn't aiming for any particular destination. I was simply trying to burn off internal energy and become calmer. But some months later, again by chance, I walked down the same lane again. That second time down Longfellow Park I stopped and looked carefully at the small and simple sign that adorned the Meeting house. I vaguely knew that the word "Friends" was the formal way of describing Quakers. A distant memory of reading something in the library of the seminary at Princeton made me mark the Meeting house on my mental map of the city, promising myself I would return. I didn't know, exactly, what Quakers were about, but I did know that I wanted to learn more.

One pleasant episode during my first fall in graduate school came at Thanksgiving. I caught a train from Boston down to Princeton and spent the holiday at the home of my undergraduate advisor. Lincoln and Sarah put on a fine repast, and we were a full table with their sons and other relatives. Quite a bit of alcohol flowed through the day, but, for a change, I imbibed in a relatively good, rather than a thoroughly compulsive, manner. The pleasures of conversation and fellowship were very real for me during that holiday weekend, and feeling the durable strength of my ties to Princeton was a boost of the sort many a first-year graduate student could use.

Despite the stress of joining a doctoral program and plunging into a new life, my first year of graduate work passed without significant health problems. I did have an unusual and remarkably intense experience while studying one afternoon. As I sat at my desk, I was suddenly overwhelmed by a deep sense of peace and warmth. But there was nothing not to like about the peace-which-passeth-understanding, and warmth in a New England winter is always good. The short but intense experience erased a powerful headache I had been suffering just as the internal "trip" began. Because the experience left me as I had been and did not recur, I marked it down as a deep and wonderful high, perhaps a mystical one, and I simply put it out of my mind.

I felt quietly steady without searing sunlight exploding in my skull, maniacal laughter or encoded messages ringing in my head, or waves of self-contempt and grief keeping me company. I was working terrifically hard in graduate courses, but, finally, I seemed to be moving over level ground rather than the uneven terrain that had defined the previous years. Just as I had during the good times at Princeton, I hoped against hope that the internal pains and demons were finally behind me. I could almost try to believe I was a normal person after all, just one who had had troubles earlier in life and who still, for some reason, wore out a pair of sturdy shoes every few months.

But the good times of my interior life were not to last long. For no apparent reason the old troubles I had known at Princeton started to come back. Although graduate school was going well, I felt the deep darkness growing within me. While I had been at Princeton it had taken months for the melancholy to fully blossom, at Harvard it took only weeks. I was confused by what was happening to me, and the pace at which it was advancing. The only response I knew how to make was to try to keep functioning. I went to classes each day, studied as long as I could concentrate, and simply soldiered on in all the ways I could find to do so.

The endless insomnia of high-energy states soon overtook me. Sleeplessness had been my nemesis at Princeton, but what I had experienced as an undergraduate soon paled compared to what enveloped me at Harvard. During the day I felt worthless and hopeless, but at night as I tossed and turned in bed through a frenzy of thought, I sank into nothing less than self-contempt. It didn't take long before I was convinced that I was an evil person. That judgment didn't rest on specific evidence, but was simply self-evident, as plain as the fact I was right-handed. I dreaded each nightfall, knowing I wouldn't sleep and my deep melancholy would escalate into true self-loathing.

As I slept less and less, exhaustion became a major factor of my existence. I've never been able to sleep during the day, so missing hours of sleep at night quickly wears down my body and brain. Although the high-energy states were strong, and essentially kept me on my feet during the days, the suffering of exhaustion was not lessened by the fact that I could stay upright and keep going. Soon a deep grief started to envelope my weary mind during the daylight as well as in the darkness of night. It felt as if my mother had suddenly died. Each evening the grief combined with a new wave of sleeplessness to explode into astounding levels of suffering, the worst I had ever known.

My spiral downward continued week after week. At one level, I thought I was being assaulted by depression, a much stronger wave than I had struggled with earlier. But this time it felt different. The illness paralyzed the best part of me, the portion of myself that could analyze the problem and look for real resources to deal with them. At that youthful stage of life, and already so sharply on the downward slope of a major mental crisis, I didn't have words for all that was happening. Like many others before me, in the state where I found myself, I didn't know where to turn. I was a young person who identified her life with excellence in intense academic work and not much else. I simply was not an adult with a lot of life experience who could understand how she might make use of medical resources for help in a rapidly worsening psychiatric downturn.

I did, however, make one good decision. In a remarkable turn of internal events, or perhaps simply by the grace of God, I didn't drink. Quitting alcohol had been something I'd worked on many times at Princeton. Somehow, this time, my resolution to not drink worked. I was helped to sobriety when I clearly and consciously realized that alcohol would kill me, as it had my grandfather some years before I was born. I knew from family lore that alcoholism led to a miserable death, and I somehow had the strength to avoid drinking even though I was in enormous pain. There's no explaining why some people are saved from addiction while others are not, but I was and am profoundly grateful for whatever factors may have been at work in my sobriety. And that remarkable blessing has lasted from my first year at Harvard down to the present.

But sober or not, my biological illness worsened and worsened. At some point, in the exhaustion of an endless night of tortured thoughts, it occurred to me that only death would relieve my suffering. Ideas about suicide present themselves to the minds of the deeply ill, and like all unbidden thoughts, they initially can be quite frightening. Still, the notion came back to me, again and again. And as time went on, the unbidden thoughts looked more and more sensible. After all, I was trapped in excruciating pain, just as I had been at Princeton, only even more strongly so. Suicide was perhaps the logical solution that had somehow eluded me when I was an undergraduate. Such became the pattern of my thinking during each long night.

Once I was suicidal, my life during the daytime was defined by fear, exhaustion, and pain. I realized I was thinking in new ways at night, different from ever before in my life, and I knew that my ideas were dangerous. During the day, I wanted to survive. But my mood and thinking would worsen with nightfall and my return to bed. I couldn't see a way forward as I endured more hours in the darkness of mental free-fall. The suffering was simply more than I could bear.

As a little girl, I had known strong night terrors. But as a graduate student my nighttime fearfulness exploded exponentially upwards in intensity. It was frustrating as a rational adult to feel my adrenalin levels increase each evening around dark. But the simple fact was that, rational or not, I experienced a fall into a chasm of fear each night. Soon the terrors were strong enough I shook in their grip, as if I had a high fever. In self-defense I bought a nightlight to keep me company. When it wasn't strong enough to lessen my fear of the dark, I left my desk lamp on all night. The bulb may have made it a fraction more difficult to fall asleep, but given the levels of night terror I was living with, I slept very little anyway.

In addition to shaking, my night experiences were characterized by the sense of rattlesnakes spread out all around me on the floor. Lying in bed I felt the presence of the rattlers coiled thickly near my bed, waiting to strike. After a few hours of tossing and turning, I always had to get up to use the toilet. But walking to the bathroom was a mental challenge because of the snakes. As usual, I talked myself through my fears as best I could. But the nightly experience of the snakes was an absolute torment.

But because I had prior experience with mental illness, I could sometimes separate myself a little bit from what was happening to me. With the fortitude I had shown earlier in life, I continued to do all I could during the day to maintain my normal existence. Although I was tremendously distracted, I did go to class. Whenever I could concentrate sufficiently, I studied. When my mental rattlesnakes were thick on the floor around my desk, I sat cross-legged or balanced my feet on the chair rungs, putting what distance I could between myself and the snakes. But intense pain has its costs even for the most disciplined person. I could no longer eat enough to maintain my weight, and I started rapidly slipping from being a thin young woman to a positively emaciated one.

As was bound to happen, the night came when I connected the idea that I was inherently evil with the possibility of suicide. Not only could my self-destruction end the horrible pain I was in, but it seemed suddenly wholly appropriate when I thought of it from the point of view of cosmic justice. Simply put, I deserved to die. Suicide was right, as well as expedient. Surely, the world and my family would be better off without me, and the problems that engulfed me would finally be addressed. That two-punch combo was a powerful new element that added to what I experienced every night.

At the start of my second year in Cambridge I had moved out of the campus dormitory and was living one subway stop away from the university. A commuter rail line came into Cambridge at that point. One night, in my usual agony during the small hours of the morning, I thought that I could go down to the railroad tracks near dawn and wait for the first commuter train to come into town. When the engine drew near, I would throw myself on the tracks. I thought that the train engineer could comfort himself that there was nothing he could have done to avoid me, since trains cannot swerve off their tracks. He could, and doubtless would, apply the brakes, but with a train behind him, he simply could not save me. I thought a bus driver would berate himself more, wondering if he could have swerved or braked more effectively. A train engineer, I hoped, could not hold himself responsible for my death.

Once the plan presented itself to me, I simply but fully accepted it. It wasn't a matter of choice, of deciding whether to act. Suicide and my plan for it simply made sense, and I was going to do it. I would die at dawn, and the world would be better off.

I felt relieved. Finally, I saw a way forward that addressed my problems and the torture in which I was living. As another hour went by, my sense of peace deepened. By four in the morning, I was entirely relieved of the ever-increasing spiral of pain tormenting me for weeks. Lying in the same bed that had so often been the scene of relentless suffering, a steady and strong calm filled me, and I was at last at ease. I breathed in that peace, grateful for it on my last night on Earth.

The next thing I knew it was a full morning and I was waking up. Looking at my clock, I saw I had missed the commuter trains coming into the station. That was my first disappointment. Taking stock of myself, I realized my sense of peace was gone, a terrible second blow. I was alive but still in the deep agony of illness.

Yet, at the same time, that little scrap of sleep inspired by my excursion into peacefulness had, for the moment, helped my tormented brain. I was not interested in killing myself at that very time. I was not interested in breakfast, but I wanted my morning cup of coffee. In short, a small sliver of better biochemistry was at work in my mind and body.

Something about the full experience of that night, the plan for my death, and the wonderful sense of peace I found in accepting it, made it possible for me to see that I didn't have to simply go to my day's classes and deny what was happening. Living through the night and what I fully expected it would have brought if I had remained awake led me to go for help from the doctors at the Harvard health service. Through a process I don't clearly remember, I was put in contact with a specific psychiatrist. I accepted an appointment, and took as my goal simply hanging on until I could see her in a couple of days.

I went to Harvard Square at the appropriate time and found the offices of the mental health group in the university health service. I met my psychiatrist, who with her silver hair looked to me like she was at least in her 60s. I told her what I had been experiencing in recent weeks. I left out the worst night, the one with the plan for the railroad tracks, as it simply seemed too awful to mention in the light of day. But, still, there was plenty enough to relate to her, including my chronic and dark feelings, weight loss, and nightly failure to sleep.

I don't remember if the psychiatrist asked if I was hearing things, but I'm sure I denied it if she did. At some deep level, I feared the messages I heard within common sounds more than anything else, and I denied even to myself the auditory experiences I sometimes had. But I related most of my other problems to the doctor, putting at her feet the other things that tormented me.

The psychiatrist told me I was suffering from depression. Once the word was spoken, I felt some relief. The psychologist at home had said I was depressed in my first year off from Princeton. I had lived through that, and life had improved. What I was dealing with wasn't, it seemed, an entirely new problem. That idea gave me hope. On the other hand, it wasn't easy to give up the level of denial that had often sustained me through difficult times. To admit that strong illness had come back to knock me off my feet once again wasn't a small matter. Sitting in the psychiatrist's office that day was another turning point in coming to grips with the idea that illness was woven into my whole existence. Once again, I had to accept that my mind was not just unusual, with some mystical trips and other odd experiences, but seriously diseased.

Seeing the psychiatrist should have been a step forward. After years of suffering, I finally made it to a psychiatrist and she recognized I was strongly ill. I went that day from being a tortured Ivy student with surprisingly little idea of what was happening, to one who was still suffering just as much as ever, but who started to have a clearer understanding that illness was a useful framework to think about what was wrong.

I saw the psychiatrist regularly. She asked me many questions focused on my childhood. That topic didn't seem relevant at all to the pain with which I was living, but there wasn't much of a choice about responding. I told her that my parents had given my brother and me a stable home life, that my upbringing was without crises and drama, that small town community life, church attendance, and good public schools had been the main features of my childhood.

The psychiatrist was quite interested in discussing my religious upbringing and beliefs. After a few sessions, she was sharing her view that my family had raised me as a fundamentalist. It was my narrow and strict religious upbringing, she said, that caused my mental illness. However, a major problem with her point of view was that my parents were not fundamentalists, nor had I been raised to be one. True, my parents were church-going Protestants, and I had gone to Sunday school and worship services each week of my youth. But in much of the country, and certainly in the small-town West, that pattern of life is not remarkable. I tried to convey those facts to the psychiatrist as best I could.

As it happened, fundamentalism was a subject in which I was fairly well versed because parts of my extended family – the parts against which my parents consciously defined themselves – were of the fundamentalist persuasion. I was therefore happy to explain to the psychiatrist the differences between mainline Protestantism and fundamentalism, noting how different my parents and I were from what she had somehow assumed. I explained that neither of my parents were inflexible fundamentalists, and I had not flirted with that approach to life. But on her side, the doctor was only willing to say I was making "unnecessary distinctions." In her mind, my religious life informed my pain, and my failure to recognize that fact doomed me to more years of suffering in the future.

I was both frustrated by the doctor's views and by the fact that she commanded the direction of our conversations. As a young person still in my early 20s, I simply couldn't keep up with the sophisticated doctor in our verbal exchanges. It soon became clear that active church membership was a status the doctor always was going to equate with illness. I had come to the doctor for help with suffering so great I was teetering on the edge of suicide, and I had been given an analysis that I thought was factually incorrect and completely unhelpful.

In some ways, even the psychiatrist admitted that she had little to offer me to help with the depth of illness I was experiencing. She didn't think I should be treated with medication. I'm not sure why that was her judgment. When I asked, rather desperately, when the grief engulfing me would let up, she said that my descent into illness would be "as long as a piece of string." From that, I gathered the state in which I found myself could go on for any length of time. Beyond that, the psychiatrist had no practical advice for me.

My attempt to get help may not have worked, but the series of appointments with the psychiatrist had somehow helped me hang on through the worst of the period of suffering. I emerged from the darkest time with very little flesh on my bones, weighing around 110 pounds –

not much for a person standing 5 foot 6 inches. Once again, I found that I was weak and scrawny, but alive and with at least a bit of fight left in me.

In a pattern of recovery that's defined my life, I soon returned to more serious engagement with my life as a student. I was far from well, but I could function enough to study and make progress in the technical classes in which I was enrolled. During the school year I lived and worked in Cambridge. During the summer, my time was spent doing fieldwork on mercury-laced hot springs in rural California, the nearest notable feature in the area being the misnamed Clear Lake.

The hot springs study was challenging but interesting. The spring waters were rich in sulfur, making them smell of rotten eggs. Earlier investigations had shown the fluids carried mercury. I took samples of the waters, the gases bubbling out of them, and the precipitates that formed around the edges of the pools. I measured such things as temperature and pH in the field, kneeling beside the smelly pools to take my measurements. Back in Cambridge, analyses showed there was gold in the precipitates. This was highly interesting to geologists, who are always on alert for anything related to precious metals, and it gave me something significant to report to my advisers at Harvard. At MIT, I did special analyses of the water where I was able to determine the exact, trace amount of gold that was dissolved in the fluid. I also measured what's termed the isotopic signature of the water itself. The results showed the fluids were deep-seated waters diluted by rainwater near the surface. In short, I measured a number of characteristics of the waters, and by luck found significant results at every turn.

The fact that the California work went so well helped me greatly as a student. I also had good luck in being a teaching assistant for the renowned paleontologist Stephen Jay Gould. Professor Gould taught a highly popular course at the freshman level. He and the class delved into many parts of geology and paleontology, exploring material at least partly through history. No one at Princeton had taught me the history of our discipline and I was delighted to learn from Gould all I could.

Although I was often absorbed in the field and laboratory work, and for one semester as a teaching assistant, I was far from well. One new internal development during that period was that I sometimes experienced full-blown panic attacks. The first one hit me one night while I was in the field in California. I awoke in the middle of the night, feeling okay. But suddenly my heart began to race faster than I had ever known it to beat. I sprang up from bed, convinced I must be having heart failure of some kind and that I would soon be unconscious and die. I ran from my room to the motel door of a fellow student traveling with me. But the time it took to do that was just enough for the worst part of the experience to pass. Encouraged, I stood still for a time and was rewarded by a gradually more slowly beating heart. In a minute, I returned to my room, convinced the strange experience would not be fatal. Later I would go through similar panic attacks in Cambridge. Still, because I'd already experienced the disorder, I never again thought I would literally die from the incredible rush of adrenalin.

One fall when I returned to Cambridge after the summer's fieldwork, I found my elderly psychiatrist had retired from the health service. I was glad to escape the stalemate that had existed between us. For some reason, perhaps because she had told me I was well again, I didn't seek out the help of another doctor. Still, in the months that followed, pieces of darkness would well up in me from time to time. Although not as terribly deep and monotonous as the worst period had been, the illness would knock me off my feet for hours or days. Then, as was bound to happen as the intensity of the illness increased, insomnia returned to stalk me at night. But between those phases of greater distress, I worked as diligently as possible and continued to progress as a doctoral student.

I do love to study. The best part of my years as a graduate student was that it was a life undergirded by studying. For at least some part of the day, seven days a week, I studied books and technical papers published in the literature of geologic research. My fellow graduate students and I sometimes felt great stress about our work, and nothing about our lives was easy. Indeed, the dropout rate for doctoral students at Harvard was very high in my day, upwards of 50%. That's an impressive proportion, in particular when one remembers that only smart and high-achieving students are admitted to graduate programs at the university. But in my case at least, I was well matched with the principal activity of a Ph.D. student. Studying was both something I knew how to do and something I loved.

I also loved to walk, and walking was a good complement to hours of studying. I had twice gone past the Quaker meeting house in my endless walks around Cambridge. One Sunday morning I walked down to Longfellow Park, took a deep breath, and went inside. Scores of Quakers were gathering in silence, taking their places on facing benches. The simple room into which people streamed was undecorated, with white walls and large but plain windows. When it began, the worship period was bathed in a deep quiet. With no music nor liturgy, the experience rested on intently listening to silence. This mode of worship was a radical departure from what I had known of church life in my childhood, but it intrigued me. I tried to both sincerely listen and also watch the Quakers around me. At a couple of points in the worship, one of the participants stood and spoke for a minute or two. What was said was just a simple observation or thought, a fragment of some larger discourse going on in the silence that underlay the gathering.

As the hour flowed along, I was drawn into the deep quiet of Quaker worship. It wasn't that it was particularly easy to listen to the silence, but I was soon impressed it was a good discipline. When I returned to the Meeting house the next Sunday, I felt a fraction more at ease. Both the silence of traditional Quaker worship and the Quakers as individuals intrigued me deeply. When an older woman explained to me there were small "Village" meetings during the week that met in people's houses, I signed up for one.

In the Village setting, I found myself getting to know individual Quakers and doing so in the intimacy of their own homes. The first meeting I attended occurred in the apartment of a smart but gentle man named Chris, a lawyer in Boston. About eight Friends gathered there. At first, people talked a bit about what was happening in their lives. Then the group became silent and worshipped in the same pattern as the larger,

Sunday meetings at the Meetinghouse. The prayer was ended with more informal talk. In short it was an intimate gathering centered on worship in a silent mode. I found it very much to my liking and went to every Village meeting that came up from then on. Through the smaller gathering I got to know Chris much better, as well as several other Quakers who were regulars at both the Village and Sunday meetings.

Soon I joined the Meeting's standing committee on social concerns, a move that introduced me to another subset of the community and to the tradition's rich social and political values. Picking up literature I found around the Meetinghouse, I read about Quaker opposition to slavery in the 1700s and 1800s, and Quakers' early support of the women's suffrage movement. Since the 1700s, Quakers have been pacifists, a viewpoint that made sense to me because my mother had raised me with respect for pacifism. I read the history of Quaker protests against wars. I also listened to Chris discuss his conscientious objection to the Vietnam War and the alternative service he did rather than being part of the American war effort of his generation. In short, my life was rapidly enriched by talking with Friends and reading about the tradition.

For me, religious life has always been tied to action. It's not enough to pray on Sundays, or even every day, if one doesn't render service to the community. Because of the life Friends showed me, I started working each week in an ecumenical soup kitchen in Harvard Square, one to which the Meeting contributed both people and money. I have always thought all Americans should have enough to eat, and the reawakening of religious life I enjoyed due to Quakers in Cambridge propelled me into the weekly work.

In the soup kitchen, I worked diligently as an assistant to the cook, chopping vegetables and stirring together recipes of bread pudding. I learned how to make a large roux at the head cook's direction and add miscellaneous boxed mixes like brownies and chocolate cake to make large pans of dessert for the 120 people who ate together at the evening meal. The kitchen part of the work was easy enough. But it was more challenging for me to sit down and eat with those who came for supper. Some of those served by the program were Cambridge's chronically mentally ill homeless, including those suffering from schizophrenia. One older woman who appeared to be in that group carried a rolled-up newspaper she used to swat insects that only she could see.

I valued the chance to be useful in the soup kitchen program, but from time to time I was staggered by the depth of the needs some of the regulars at the suppers clearly displayed. In my own confused way, I emphatically denied to myself that I was as ill as many who came to the evening meal, even as part of me wondered if I would end up in a similar situation as the woman who compulsively swatted imaginary insects.

But although it wasn't easy to volunteer at the soup kitchen, it was important to me. I felt truly called by faith to help those in the city without enough to eat. I learned quite a bit in my role as assistant to the cook. When he went away on vacation one week in the summer, I worked all day making the complete meal, laboring about 8 hours over it so I only had to do one thing at a time. I was proud – and relieved – when all 120 people were served what I had prepared.

Quaker meetings, silent and contemplative prayer, and service work at the soup kitchen all enriched my life. Soon I had good friends in the Meeting as well as from the soup kitchen staff. In time, after studying Quaker history and the writings of significant British and American Quakers, it was natural and right to join the Meeting officially. Thus, although I was suffering strongly at times due to painful internal states, I had also found the energy to expand my life. I was – and to this day still am – blessed by that aspect of my years in Cambridge. Doing soup kitchen work and going to worship meetings felt right, in large part because I had been raised within church life. In that way, the manner my parents had raised me in the rural Northwest led to an enrichment of my life in Cambridge.

My life was also broadened when I moved into an apartment in Somerville to share it with three Harvard graduate students outside my department. Sarah was in classics, her boyfriend Doug was in biochemistry, as was Eric. We shared the rent and bought groceries in common, sometimes cooking for each other and sometimes cooking for a subset of the collective or just for ourselves. The apartment was made up of the second and third stories of a small, old house, built in the backyard of another house so it was off the street. Sarah and I put up clear plastic over the windows in the little living room, but it remained drafty all winter long. My bedroom was on the third floor, farthest from the furnace in the basement, and it was cold during the heating season.

More emotionally challenging for me was that the place was dark. The windows were small because the house was old, and the lighting in the stairwell in particular was inadequate. But what the apartment lacked in terms of physical amenities, it made up for due to the people living there. Sarah and Eric, in particular, became my good friends. We talked and laughed together over common meals, and shared notes about the peculiarities of the Harvard faculty who dominated our lives as students. Sarah was always studying ancient languages and literature, but in her free time, she wrote poetry and spent time with Doug. The two married while we were graduate students but they continued to live in the apartment with Eric and me. For his part, Eric put his free time into Jewish cultural and religious life. I learned a lot about Jewish holidays from watching him go through them as the year's cycle played out. Eric was soon dating a graduate student named Esther, and the two married after we all had left Harvard.

But the positive parts of my life could not protect me from illness. In time, the darkness returned. I could feel myself sliding downward, at first week by week and then at a speed so rapid I could register the descent on a daily basis. I was in free fall in a dark mine shaft once again, and I had no way to stop what was happening. Desperate to help myself before I became suicidal, I went to Harvard's emergency room. The rattlesnakes were swarming the floor of the ER as I tried to convey to a doctor what was happening in my life.

Thankfully, he listened and checked me into the small hospital that Harvard maintained next to the university in Harvard Square, promising I'd see a psychiatrist in the morning. Bright and early the next day, a younger psychiatrist came to see me. He was quite different from the sharp-edged older woman I had known in the Harvard Health Service. For one thing, the younger doctor spoke softly and kindly. As soon as he introduced himself, he asked if he would do, or if I wanted to exchange him for another psychiatrist. I assured him I thought he was a keeper.

The new psychiatrist had to take my history and cover some of the same ground as the woman doctor had earlier done. But the new man showed no real interest in my religious upbringing or my life in Cambridge as a Quaker. He did, however, broach a new idea for me to consider. I could be helped, he patiently and quietly assured me, by anti-depressant medications. This approach to mental illness was the modern view informed by science. Because I was a student of science, surely, I could understand what I was experiencing was a chemical imbalance in my brain, one that could be treated by medication just as diabetics and asthmatics treat their condition with appropriate drugs. Without ever criticizing the elderly woman doctor, my new psychiatrist made it clear that her approach to mental illness was of the past, while he was working in the present.

My new doctor's approach was, indeed, in keeping with the times, and I took in the message of the gentle psychiatrist as best I could. He was a thoroughly professional doctor, and I appreciated his attitude toward me. But although I looked up to him, I also resisted the idea that medication was all I needed. It wasn't that my life had been pristinely drug-free. I had abused alcohol off and on for years at Princeton, and I knew it. But I hoped all of that was behind me, and I didn't want to exchange one set of drugs for another. If nothing else, I was a profoundly stubborn young woman and wanted to get better on my own. At the core, my objections to anti-depressants probably were not rational. But they were clear and strong, and I knew I simply didn't want to take the drugs. So, politely, I declined.

The young psychiatrist was professional enough that he didn't argue with me. I continued to see him every week or two and describe my moods. My outlook varied, generally ranging from grim-but-livable to downright life-threatening. At some point, as was bound to happen, I simply stopped sleeping. Night after night I was awake, with a surge in nocturnal energy that hit the highest point it has ever been in my life. My interior darkness was my closest companion, and self-destruction was not far from me. My mind was filled with a deep grief. I lost weight by the handfuls, then lost still more. At my lowest ebb in graduate school, I weighed 104 pounds, not nearly enough for an active and outdoorsy woman. Weeks of suffering slid into months. Sleeping just two or three hours per night, my exhaustion mounted and my thinking deteriorated. Off and on I went back to the hospital for rest and to protect myself from the worst of what was engulfing me.

As with any sort of chronic experience, the mind adapts as best it can to what engulfs it. One habit I adopted to combat the night terrors was to think of several positive ideas in the early evening. Some nights I even talked over this strategy with my Quaker friends.

"Help me think of three good things," I would say, often over the telephone as I prepared to go to bed.

I would then formulate my positive ideas, three pieces of driftwood onto which I could cling at night to stop myself from drowning in the darkness. The ideas ranged from simple aspects of my daily life – like having good friends in New England and my loving family back home in the Pacific Northwest – to more abstract ideas like progress with my academic work. After enumerating my "three good things" I would feel a tiny bit more able to face the terrors of the on-coming night. Still, no amount of strategizing could change the fact I was going to be tormented by rattlesnakes and swimming with grief for hours in the darkness.

Even the warm cocoon created by Harvard's hospital could not save me from my troubles. Many nights I stayed there I simply couldn't fall asleep. When I grew weary of tossing and turning in the hospital bed, I'd get up. Clad only in my pajamas, I often spent the small hours of the morning pacing back and forth in the long hallway of the facility. The hall had a window at either end. Looking out at Cambridge's many lights burning brightly in the night marked a brief moment that interrupted my pacing. Then I'd turn around and head back down the hall, striding or stumbling as I went depending how advanced was my exhaustion.

One night my suffering was so extreme that I silently called out to God for help as I paced. While at an intellectual level I don't necessarily hold with petitionary prayer, I was in so much agony that night that I cried out in the quiet darkness at the end of the hall, begging the Almighty for help. I heard a strong and clear voice in that moment of deep torment. In ringing tones, it spoke to me, saying in the words of scripture: "My grace is sufficient for thee."

I was glad – and amazed – to have an audible reply from the darkness. I recognized the words from Paul's second letter to the Corinthians. Like Paul, I had begged for help and been promised not direct aid, but grace instead. But that night I wanted healing and release from pain, not God's grace. Although I treasured the words I had so clearly and distinctly heard, in a practical sense my prayer had not been answered. There was nothing to do but keep pacing.

I didn't tell the psychiatrist that I had heard the voice of God. I viewed it as a religious matter, something like the mystical experiences I had known since childhood. At some level, I knew a secular doctor at Harvard might characterize it differently, and I didn't want to deal with some diagnosis I understood only vaguely that hinged on auditory hallucinations. A psychiatrist, I suspected, might well think that hearing God speak directly to me in clear words wasn't so different from the invisible insects that tormented the schizophrenic homeless woman who came for meals at the soup kitchen. I didn't want to be like her, so I didn't tell the doctor what I had heard in the hallway of the hospital.

I somehow rallied from that long night, got a little rest, and went home. But when awful suffering returned, I went back to the hospital. The hospital began to function like a revolving door in my life, taking me in when my moods were most intensely dangerous when the rattlesnakes were thick on the floor. After days or weeks of the most intense pain, some change would occur and I'd sleep a little more. That was always a great restorative, and I would be able to think more clearly. In those phases in the hospital, I sometimes worked on tabulating my research data. I even wrote longhand versions of what would become parts of my doctoral dissertation while I was hospitalized.

As a regular in the hospital scene at Harvard, I came to understand that the other patients in the institution were quite a diverse group. Older faculty members were doing short stays for a procedure or some other specific event in their lives. There was one young man – a long term resident – with full-blown AIDS. And then there were those of us who were reasonably sound in body but were psych patients.

One day I was sitting in the day-room, an area with a table, some soft chairs, and a good view towards the Charles River. The room was the only alternative to sitting in individual patients' rooms. Several young people, including one who had just joined us at night, were in the room that morning. A psychiatrist entered and started to speak with the newest arrival. She asked general questions at first and got matter-of-fact answers. Soon, however, she focused on what had happened the previous night. It became clear from the conversation that the man had swallowed a handful of pills and been brought to the ER by his friends. He was full of remorse about the whole event, volunteering to the doctor he didn't want to distress his friends as he just had done.

As the young man and the psychiatrist spoke, the other patients in the room got up and left one by one. I could see from where I was sitting that one of them shook his head as he did so. But I remained where I was. I was neither embarrassed to overhear the conversation, nor surprised it was happening. As someone living with suicidal thoughts each night, I could empathize with the young man.

The doctor next steered the conversation to the young man's family – and the fact they needed to be told about what he had done and where he now was. At that point, the student started to cry. Gentle tears were soon followed by harsh sobs. His tears made me think he might prefer a measure of privacy, so I left the day-room as he wept. From the outside looking in, student life at Harvard may seem an enviable existence – and of course, all students enrolled in such an institution are deeply fortunate. But, at least as some of us can testify, Harvard can also be hell on Earth.

On and on the cycles of greater and lesser inner torment went. In the end I checked myself into the hospital more times than I could count. After my stays had run their course, I'd check myself out and go back to the old and drafty shared apartment. But my upswings were always short-lived. In several weeks I would fall back into a suicidal and sleepless state, losing what little strength and weight I had managed to build up. Soon I realized that I gained ground on the upswings only very slowly, while I could lose what small shred of health I might possess with breathtaking rapidity. Made desperate by yet another downswing, I changed my mind about trying anti-depressants. The psychiatrist immediately wrote me a prescription for Prozac, and I went home to try it.

I clearly remember the three days I tried to take the drug. I had a good attitude about the medication when I swallowed the first capsule. I wanted Prozac to help me. I was, after all, a scientist, and I could easily imagine that some significant chemical imbalance in my brain was distorting my whole life. But the medication led to an almost electrical surge of hellish energy that flooded my whole body. The treatment was worse than the disease.

It was back to the drawing board. I struggled, as best I could, to live through waves of anguish and suffering and scores of rattlesnakes on the floor around me. Seasons came and went. One typical night occurred on a pleasant spring evening. It was a Saturday, and a Quaker friend named Cliff and I had gone to an early movie screening in Harvard Square. Before the film was over, however, I felt full night terrors exploding within me. Soon I was shaking violently from head to foot. Cliff and I walked to Harvard's E.R. just a block from where we had seen the film. I was shaking uncontrollably when a young doctor came to see me.

"Your blood pressure is through the roof," he said. "What drugs have you been doing this evening?"

I explained I'd taken no street drugs of any kind, and had not had any alcohol. But again, the doctor pressed me to tell him what drugs were in my system. At that point, Cliff spoke up, assuring the doctor that whatever I was experiencing was coming from within me due to natural biology rather than being artificially induced.

"I shake quite a few nights," I explained. "I just get so afraid."

Looking back at all the contact I had with ER doctors and psychiatrists during my Harvard years, it is puzzling that I was so poorly diagnosed. But the doctors continued to see my problems as caused by simple depression, at least that's what they said to me. The obvious mental and physical high-energy states I lived with most nights didn't fit easily with the diagnosis of depression, but I was far too naïve – and too ill – to press the doctors to do better diagnostic work. So, on I suffered, with night terrors worthy of ancient Greek sagas, chasms of fear-producing levels of suffering that kept my life at risk month after month.

I don't understand why I lived through the terrible pain I experienced at Harvard. Nor can I understand how I intermittently made progress on my schoolwork. All I know is that I poured my energy into my studies whenever I could function. Doing my dissertation research became my highest goal, one I may have valued more than life itself. In any event, one thing is certain: when I wasn't shaking or walking around Cambridge trying to blow off energy, I was trying to do my schoolwork. Thankfully, my intermittent efforts were enough to make progress toward my degree.

Despite my brain's regrettable talent for plunging me into suffering, I have a powerful resilience. When all seemed lost and life was slipping through my fingers at Harvard, for no particular reason I could see, I would simply start to do a bit better. Suicidal desire would melt away like late winter snow. Although I was still deeply ill, I would begin to function better as a graduate student. Somewhere in the fog of deep illness I completed my laboratory work at MIT and produced further rounds of data at Harvard for my dissertation.

Step by step, I made progress toward the goal of leaving Harvard, and, I deeply hoped and prayed, of finding myself on firmer ground internally. Maybe after my education was complete, I could feel more as I had when I was still a young child, and less like I had in all the intervening years. It wasn't a hope grounded in rationality, but it informed my spirits on my good days, and it gave me part of what I needed to keep putting one foot in front of the other.

But the spring I was working to complete my degree brought back all my usual pains and distress. Although I made progress with my academic work, I became terribly ill. The strongest of the demons were reignited. After I defended my dissertation work and turned it into the appropriate university office, I earned my Ph.D., but I also checked myself back into the hospital. The time had come for me to try more anti-depressants, and to do so from the relative safety of an institutional environment.

With no more school work to do, I took the trial of anti-depressant medications as my life task. One by one, the doctor and I experimented with four different drugs. Each made me ill, either with physical side effects too strong to tolerate or – like the Prozac had done – with mental effects that were actually worse than what naturally ailed me. While trying a medication called Trazadone, I started to run a temperature, an event fully documented because I was in a hospital and my vital signs were regularly recorded.

My psychiatrist at first denied Trazadone could be causing the fever – no such side effect was noted for it in the Physician's Desk Reference, the bible of medications and their effects. Because I was in a hospital running a fever and the doctor couldn't imagine I was being made ill by the drug I was taking, he tested me for a wide range of infectious diseases. When all the results came back negative, he sat down to talk with me. I reported to him that while the tests were being run, I had spoken long distance on the telephone with my mother. She had looked up Trazadone in a consumer's guide publication she happened to have. The book said the drug could indeed cause elevated body temperatures. To his credit, the Harvard psychiatrist took what my mother had relayed to me seriously. He ordered the medication stopped. In 24 hours, my fever went away. I agreed to take the Trazadone again in the spirit of giving the matter the best of tests. Sure enough, the fever returned, but disappeared again when I stopped the drug for the second and final time. With that, the doctor was willing to cross Trazadone off the list of what might be possible for me.

More medication experiments followed. Again and again, the drugs proved unhelpful or down-right harmful. By August, I had to face up to my situation as the days dwindled away that the student health insurance policy would cover me. I was far too ill to work, and I was penniless. With the support of Clifford, the good Quaker friend, I reluctantly but resignedly filled out the paperwork to apply for welfare. But one night, I had a simple yet strong brainwave. Since I couldn't support myself, I had to ask my parents if they would take me in. I called them, and they agreed I could come home and live in their house. As always, they said they were sorry I was ill, but they would be glad to see me again even for an open-ended stay. So it was that, for the third time, I returned to the Pacific Northwest in a state of deep illness.

CHAPTER 4:

BOOKS AND GEOLOGY

I returned home from New England a basket case. I weighed barely more than 100 pounds. I tossed and turned at night rather than sleeping. I cried regularly and bitterly, but the tears brought no emotional release. It was a burden to eat, to invest the emotional energy to relate to people, and do the simple tasks of daily living. I felt like I was at the funeral of a dear friend or close relative. Always, both day and night, there were rattlesnakes on the floor.

The torment of the snakes deserves some further explanation. There are two types of rattlesnakes in my life. The first are the real ones. These include the reptiles I occasionally meet at home in the inland Northwest in the warm-weather months when walking my dog for miles along the well-named Snake River. As it moves through the southern boundary of the county where my hometown lies, the river flows at the bottom of a stunning canyon that would be a National Park if it were located somewhere in the East. The base of the canyon has a considerably warmer climate than the plateau that lies more than 1800 feet above it.

The lower reaches of the canyon make an ideal home for rattlesnakes. They warm themselves on the dark rocks during cool mornings and slither freely around during hot afternoons. I was to meet larger flesh-and-blood rattlers when I did geologic research around Grand Coulee in north-central Washington. As a native Westerner, I stoned a few rattlers to death when I was young, acting on the not-so-progressive principle that a good rattler is a dead rattler. I've long since given up that habit, partly perhaps because I have broader ecological perspectives in old age, or mostly because it's easier to live and let live.

Although many people I know fear rattlesnakes, they don't understand half the problem the reptiles pose for me. I've met more rattlers in the regular world than I can count, but they've not been important beyond the brief times I've spent in their presence. However, the snakes of my mind cause me real hardship and suffering. For most of the days that have made up the past 40 years, I have had the clear sense that rattlesnakes are near my feet on the floor. I don't literally see them, but I feel their presence just as strongly as I feel there are people around me at a worship service in the church.

Unlike flesh-and-blood rattlers, my mental rattlesnakes come in swarms, coiling themselves near my feet a half dozen at a time. The snakes my mind creates are so close to sinking their fangs into my shins that I sometimes pick up my feet and tuck them underneath me on my chair. That's not an easy position in which to sit, particularly the older I get and the more knee pain I live with, but sometimes I do almost anything to find a scrap of relief from the stress brought on by the nearness of my chronic companions.

The rattlesnakes that keep me close company sometimes trip my hair-trigger adrenalin system. Even though I think that the snakes are not real, their powerful presence near me can precipitate physical jolts of fear. Naturally, when I had even a mild sense there were rattlesnakes on my office floor, it was difficult to concentrate on my work. When I'm in bed at night, the snakes can be a clear presence on my bedroom carpet. Sometimes the venomous reptiles keep me in a state of such chronic anxiety I have to take ulcer medicine to combat the stress they inspire.

The worse the degree of mental illness I'm experiencing, the clearer the presence of the snakes. In my darkest times, when my life is at stake, the snakes come up on my bed at night around my feet. I can do nothing to protect myself from them except spring up and flee. When I was young and still able to do long, nocturnal ramblings, I would try to run or walk away from the rattlers, covering the ground outdoors until my blistered feet sometimes literally bled inside my shoes. But no matter how many miles I put behind me, the snakes always kept up. I am well and truly wed to the rattlers; when things are bad there is simply nowhere I can go that they do not immediately follow.

When I came home to my parents' house after graduate work, the full range of my symptoms tormented me. But they were hardly my only problem. Among the difficulties I faced was that I was so weak I couldn't blow off my dark energy via 10-mile walks. Indeed, when I got home and caught up on jet lag, my first walk was literally around the block on which my parent's house stood – that was enough at the time to count as significant exertion. I thought about suicide frequently, which made me mortally afraid in my better moments and increased the adrenalin levels in my bloodstream. At times I was inconsolable because I simply couldn't see how I could continue to bear up under the physical and emotional suffering that engulfed me. In short, I was much more deeply ill than when I had previously returned to the Northwest after either my freshman or junior years in college.

Still, as always, I showed some basic talent at putting one foot in front of the other. I tried to eat, sleep, and do the simple things of ordinary life like reading the morning newspaper. I kept a close eye on my thoughts and did what I could to avoid falling down suicidal mineshafts. I was often tormented by the rattlesnakes on the floor, but I talked myself through the experiences, trying to use the reasoning sector of my brain against the rest of my mind. I knew the snakes were not real, and I lectured myself about that fact seventy times per day. I longed at every moment for less pain in my life. My hopes, however, were dashed by my experience, even in the safety of my family home. Still, I broke down everything I could into small parts, taking just one more step at a time, and I always tried hard to move forward. In that one sense only – the basic fact that I didn't give up – I was undefeated.

My parents worked hard every day to take care of me. They were fantastically gentle and kind. The period in question fell before my father's retirement, so he was still working, but my mother was at home with me during the days. She tried to fix something I would like for lunch, or suggest I accompany her to the store in the afternoon. If I cried, she would sit with me. If I carried the groceries from the car, she made sure to thank me for my help.

In the evenings both of my parents and I spent time together. Because

I couldn't abide watching television, we read aloud to fill the evening hours. It's impressive to me now that I look back at it that, night after night, both my parents found the time and the energy to sit in the living room with me and read. We explored together the novels of Jane Austin, of Dickens, and the Brontë sisters. The reading sessions helped pass the time, and I'm sure they were emotionally important to me because they expressed my parent's unqualified love for their terribly tormented daughter.

Simply put my father and mother encouraged me at every level and spoke to me about the good things my future might still hold. But only their love coupled with their hope for their daughter, gave their words any power. The fact was that only deeply committed people could find the energy to sustain real faith in me in light of how poorly I was faring. The simple truth was that I was almost an invalid. Day after day I accomplished nothing more than keeping myself alive. All the objective evidence of the time pointed toward a lifetime of disability and inactivity, with mental illness keeping me in a fully crippled state.

Then, perhaps by the grace of God, I started to write.

I remember exactly where I began what has turned out to be the long project of becoming a professional writer. One afternoon, about a month after I returned home, I walked to the student union on the Washington State University (WSU) campus next to my parents' house. In my condition, just being in public and away from my home took a measure of courage. Reaching the student union – a walk of half a dozen blocks – was an accomplishment. Using the change in my pocket I bought a cup of coffee in the cafeteria and sat down at a table to rest. I happened to have a pen with me. Out of idleness, I took a paper napkin and began to daydream about fragments of a fictional story set in Cambridge, Mass.

I don't know why my thoughts went in that particular direction. Perhaps the nightly reading sessions with my parents helped trigger ideas about a tale of my own. I'm sure I had never thought of writing any fiction prior to that moment, and it was odd even to consider such a task given the wretched levels of suffering that engulfed me. But daydream I did, making a few marks on the paper napkin as I did so. The first thoughts that came to my mind were about a heroine who was a middle-aged woman and head of the Quaker meeting I had joined in Cambridge. I began to put down a few facts about her. Quickly, I came to think the story could unfold in the framework of a murder mystery.

Perhaps it wasn't such a surprise my day-dream took the form of thinking about a mystery story. As a kid, I had enjoyed reading who-done-its. While I was in middle school, I had read several Agatha Christie mysteries, with the Miss Marple stories being my favorite. As I grew a bit older and more sophisticated, I graduated to the mysteries penned by Dorothy Sayers starring Lord Peter Wimsey. But until that day in the student union, looking down at my paper napkin, I had never considered writing a mystery of my own – nor of writing a book of any kind. Still, as I sat in isolation at my little table in the cafeteria, fully tormented in body and mind, a cluster of ideas came to me. In self-defense, more than anything else, I jotted down more notes on my napkin. When I finished my coffee there was nothing to do but use my remaining strength to walk home. But I carried the napkin with me, and once ensconced in my parent's house again, I started to pen a few lines that opened a simple story set in and around the Friends Meeting I valued so deeply.

There's an irony, of course, in using a pacifist community as the backdrop for any story that revolves around an act of violence. But Quakers are sinners just as much as anyone else, and an individual Quaker can surely commit any act more mainstream people do. Besides, murder mysteries are pieces of fiction, not a recounting of facts. And my story, I was sure, was just an exercise to give me something to do. In the privacy of my own head, there was no harm in thinking how fictional Quakers might be caught up in the tangles of a murder mystery.

Looking back at it, it's not surprising I started to write about Friends Meeting at Cambridge. I missed my Quaker friends greatly, thinking of them each day with real longing. To be sure, I had come back to my childhood home voluntarily. But I didn't return home because I actually wanted to leave my life in New England, only because I was too ill to work. Each day at home I missed Quaker life and working in the soup kitchen where I had labored in Cambridge. Most of all, I simply missed my good friends, like Cliff, who had accompanied me to the Harvard ER on the night I was shaking so violently. Writing about Quakers was the next best way I had of being with them.

As the fall progressed, so did my story. At some point, I started reading my manuscript aloud to my parents during our evening sessions. They encouraged me to continue with my efforts. Having nothing else to occupy myself, I wrote some each day, extending the story time and time again. When I was too distracted and tormented to write, I tried to walk a little bit or I talked with my mother. But whenever I could, I sat down with the story and tried to add a couple of pages to it.

In the early winter, I sent my growing manuscript to one of my Harvard housemates, the classics major who wrote poems in her free time. Sarah very kindly combed through it at the word-by-word level, editing as she went and explaining in notes why she recommended certain changes. I also got editorial input from my parents. Gradually, the work improved a bit, and then a bit more. It surprised me that the project could move forward because I didn't know what I was doing, and I had no outline or plan for developing the story. But, just by dint of my working at it, the simple tale unfolded chapter by chapter. Writing a murder mystery felt a lot like reading one – it just took much longer.

It's easy to romanticize writing. But in my experience, writing murder mysteries is simply a task any compulsive person can take on, like establishing a large garden in the backyard. I doggedly slogged on with my project as the fall dissolved into winter, and the winter then melted into spring. When the flowers were blooming around my parents' house, I was finished, having produced a book-length story with at least the general appearance of a beginning, a middle, and an end. When I read the last few pages aloud to my parents, we discussed what I could potentially do with the manuscript. On a whim, and using connections with a former student of my father who had written several spy thrillers,

I contacted a literary agent in New York. The agent was Clyde Taylor, to whom I sent a query letter and then the manuscript. I had little hope that a professional person Back East would see any value in my story, but simply sending it to New York helped me to feel I had wrapped up the adventures of my Quaker heroine.

Unfortunately, my health had not improved as I labored on the murder mystery. I was just as ill when I finished it as when I had begun. It was staggering to think that a whole school year had gone by in such a wretched state. Whereas my earlier retreats to the Northwest had been enough to help me heal and start life anew, my first-year home after graduate school had actually done nothing for me. From time to time, I heard what seemed to me to be messages in something like Morse Code, and on a daily basis, my mental rattlesnakes surrounded me.

A couple of weeks after I mailed my manuscript to New York I got a letter from Clyde. He said he liked the book very much, but he had been unable to call me because I had not given him my phone number. He asked me to call him in New York. When I did so, he was warm and encouraging, volunteering that he could try to sell the manuscript if I signed up as an author with his agency, Curtis Brown Ltd. Having no other offers, I agreed. Just a few weeks later he called to say he could sell the manuscript to a division of Random House as part of a three-book series. The advances were modest tokens, compensating me at about the level of the minimum wage for all the time I had spent writing. But modest or not, there were at least advances to discuss. I was both delighted and astounded by my good fortune with respect to both acquiring an agent and finding out that I would become a published author.

The good news from New York boosted my spirits. The fact that I agreed to produce two more books helped concentrate my mind. Clearly, I had my work cut out for me. One immediate question was whether I wanted the books to come out under my name or a pen name. I was still young enough to feel shy about displaying any work of mine in a fully public venue, so I quickly opted for the emotional safety of a pen name.

Naturally, given that the story was about Quakers, a British-sounding name seemed most appropriate. Talking it over with my mother one day she reminded me that her mother – my maternal grandmother – had been called Irene Allen as a child. That was an English-sounding name, and one I liked. I wrote to my ninety-year-old grandmother, asking if it would be possible for me to use her birth name on my books. She happily agreed, so my career as Irene Allen got underway. I immediately began to write the second book and had a good start on it when the first one came out. When that initial tale was reviewed favorably in The New York Times, I blessed Clyde's name, as did my parents, I was sure.

The second year after my return home went by largely like the first. Nights continued to be painful and difficult, with the tortures of insomnia and dark thoughts waiting for me when I turned out the lights in my childhood bedroom. On truly bad nights, I shook with grief and terror. My parents had to help me think of three good things in the evening so I could arm myself with something positive before going to bed. And although the days were generally better than the nights, I lost many a morning or afternoon to simple but profound mood swings that dropped me into the darkness.

Throughout this whole period, I was too ill to look for full-time work. True, some days I was in half-decent shape and could have done something useful for an employer, at least in a routine job. But I couldn't last through an 8-hour effort, and many days I wasn't up to doing anything at all. Because I could never predict what the morning would bring, I seemed to be fully stalemated in the working world. Writing was perhaps the only thing I could do, simply because I could do it whenever I could function enough to sit at a keyboard and walk away from it when my demons were strong.

I did gradually experience some improvement in my symptoms as that second year unfolded. I slowly grew in physical strength, putting on some needed weight. I started to sleep marginally better, which helped everything all around. Capitalizing on those changes, I found I was able to write up my dissertation in the form of articles for technical journals.

Again, writing tasks were possible when so much else was not because I could write during my brief better times, and simply ignore my writing work when I was shaking with fear or grief.

I also started talking with faculty members in the geology department at Washington State University, the land-grant university just a block from my parent's house. I had literally played on the campus lawns as a child, and I knew the sprawling campus like I did the back of my hand. I talked with one of the geology faculty members in my field and the department agreed to give me a desk and a mailbox. I had no income from the department, but being associated with it gave me stationery to use when I submitted my dissertation research to technical journals.

One challenge I had to face beyond my medical problems was that my small hometown had no Quaker meetinghouse. Because of that, I started attending worship services at a church that stood a block from my parents' home. The church is Episcopalian, meaning its worship services are based on the liturgy in the Book of Common Prayer, making it as "high church" as we Protestants can get. While on the opposite end of formality from a silent Quaker meeting, I found a crucial element in common between Episcopal worship and the Friends meeting style. Both groups have designed what they do on Sunday mornings to create a strong sense of the holiness of worship.

I have nothing against the in-between denominations like the Methodists, Presbyterians, and the Congregationalists. But worship meetings in such churches often have the business-like tone of a school board meeting. They are simply not designed to create a clear break in the mood of the mind, as does, for example, worship in a cathedral with its ritual music and stained glass windows that take people beyond themselves. What initially took me back to the Episcopal services week after week was the experience of worship itself, the seeking after the holiness of the experience of God's presence among us. Soon, however, I started to make friends with individual Episcopalians, giving me a second reason to show up at the weekly worship hour.

As that second year at home gradually passed, I progressed on several fronts. I started to be able to go for significant walks, as I had when I was younger and living in the East. I could concentrate longer and relate to other people more easily. I continued to work on the next murder mystery manuscript and had the energy to look for a part-time job. The only work I could immediately find was driving a van to the Spokane airport which lies 80 miles to the north of my hometown. I worked for the van service part-time, doing only day-time runs when they were available. But the experience was good, forcing me to go out in public and deal with a wide variety of people with different needs. I was the only Harvard Ph.D. I knew who was earning the minimum wage as a driver, but I also was glad to have the job as a test of my growing strength.

Slowly, in fits and starts, I improved as more time passed. Journal articles and another mystery book accumulated to my credit. Still, what progress I made came only in patches. My life seemed to be characterized by taking two steps forward, and then one step back. I made it through the most difficult days only due to the wall-to-wall support of my parents. Another year slowly passed in a roughly similar fashion as the earlier ones. I could do marginally more work, but the ups and downs I went through were still enormous, and the tough times could wipe out the incremental progress that accumulated so slowly. I wasn't a full invalid any longer, but I was still decidedly crippled.

Looking back, I don't know how my parents found the time and the emotional energy to support and encourage me as much as they did. In short, they put everything else in their lives on hold and tried their level best to care for me. They shared my joy when a manuscript was finished and accepted in New York. They also persevered with me through the bad nights when – for no reason at all – I'd take a downturn, crying and shaking all over again. Without them, I believe the rattlesnakes of my mind would have overwhelmed me. One thing is certain: more steadfast love than what they gave me during that long and difficult time I cannot imagine.

Of course, at times I was frustrated by the fact I was living like a child in the very house where I'd grown up. But the brutal fact was that I had no money and was too ill to work significantly. As I saw it, my options were to stay with my parents or take up the life on the streets I'd seen people leading around the soup-kitchen where I had worked in Cambridge. Given only those two choices, I knew where I wanted to be. And my parents never spoke to me about what it cost them – financially or emotionally – to care for me.

The long and hard slog through which my parents aided me was one I undertook without medication. My parents and I assumed I was fighting depression, as depression was the only diagnosis I'd ever been given. But I'd tried so many anti-depressants at Harvard all three of us didn't hold out much hope that medication could help me. Looking back, I probably should have tried to see a psychiatrist after I got home. Mental illness was clearly ruining my life, and it makes sense for the mentally ill to seek the care of physicians trained in psychiatric conditions. But I had no health insurance or money, and seeing a medical specialist looked mightily expensive. Beyond that, I knew of no psychiatrist in my hometown – the nearest psych clinics that we knew about were an hour's drive to the south or an hour and a half away toward the north. Finally, I had been cared for at Harvard by two psychiatrists, yet I had remained deeply ill. Perhaps it's no wonder my parents and I never decided to get me into the care of a psychiatrist, deciding to muddle along only with the power of family love.

But profoundly ill though I still was, I also slowly gained physical and emotional strength. My progress may have been slow, but there was indeed progress. Gradually things improved on all fronts. With my parents' encouragement, I started to spend more time hanging out in the geology department of WSU. One day the chairman saw me and asked if I would be interested in teaching the summer session of freshman geology. I readily agreed to the project. A faculty member normally in charge of the freshman geology program then took me under his wing. Larry Davis was a warm-hearted man who perhaps saw I had some potential if I could get past the insecurity I felt due to the severity of my health problems. With Larry's help, I got ready to teach the summer session class.

From that modest beginning, my efforts in the Geology Department expanded. The Dean of Science, it turned out, wanted the geology department to develop a new and innovative course for non-science majors at the freshman level. No one on the faculty wanted to do the work required to create such a course, but I told the chairman I'd be glad to put my shoulder to that particular wheel. I had been a teaching assistant at Harvard for the famous paleontologist Stephen J. Gould, and there I'd been exposed to many interesting tales about the history of geology. With those ideas as a backdrop, I started to develop a new course at WSU that would show students how science actually worked, rather than just telling them many facts about the natural world.

I was frustrated with my new teaching efforts because there wasn't anything useful I could find students at the freshman level to read for the course I envisioned. While many textbooks were published for freshman geology classes, they were all variations on one model, namely broad surveys of the vocabulary of the whole field. The textbooks were and are good, but they don't help students understand how science works in practice or what scientists do in their lives as researchers. Because I couldn't find any published books that would be useful for my course, I started to write a manuscript of my own to fill what I thought was a significant gap in what was commercially available.

The writing project moved along quite briskly. The fact that I had a couple of murder mysteries under my belt may not have been directly useful, but I think the hours I'd spent at the keyboard turning out those books had taught me some basics about shaping paragraphs and chapters. Once I had a pile of manuscript pages assembled, I looked around for someone able to be an informal editor for me. Back in my Princeton days I'd been very impressed with geologist Sheldon Judson, and I'd corresponded with him a bit after I returned home. Sheldon had written a series of geology textbooks over the years, all published by Prentice Hall. I asked him if he'd be willing to read my manuscript chapters and give them a critical going-over. Fortunately for me, Sheldon had retired and had time available. He agreed to help.

To say that Sheldon proved a good editor is an understatement. He recognized I was trying to write a different textbook from those on the market, and he immediately got on board with the project. A skillful writer, he edited my prose at a detailed level, moving my efforts in a better direction time and time again. He also provided emotional support, praising me enough to keep me at the keyboard trying to improve. In short, he was a first-rate teacher, even if he was 3,000 miles away from where I sat at my desk in my parents' household.

When I felt the manuscript was complete, I photocopied it and started to have my students read it. I also talked to several textbook salesmen who came by the department. Perhaps out of politeness, a couple of them agreed to take a copy of the manuscript and give it to their editors in New York. I waited for a possible response, not expecting very much but eager to hear what textbook editors operating at the national level would think of my non-traditional textbook. One of the editors responded to me, namely Holly Hodder of W.H. Freeman and Co. Holly said, she loved my alternative approach to teaching freshmen, and she wanted to publish the book. Once again, my good fortune in publishing my prose surprised and delighted me. Over the next year, the book was polished, and simple illustrations were developed in New York to grace the pages of what became a small paperback book. As usual, my royalties worked out to be about the minimum wage for all the time I put into the effort, but I was glad to have any remuneration for my writing.

As the small textbook came out, I was starting to build a life for myself. Then, just as everything was going clearly better, a tsunami of mental illness swept over me once again. It was summer when the dark energy surged all around me. My parents were out of town on a road-trip to the Midwest, so I was alone in the house – a factor that didn't cause my troubles but that certainly didn't help me cope with the severity of what I was experiencing.

With dread, I watched the symptoms of my suffering grow, and then grow still more. Soon I was having enormous difficulty sleeping. Both night and day there seemed to be rattlesnakes on the floor around me. Weight began to melt off my body as I quickly fell back into the hell I'd been living in when I left Harvard. Words cannot express how frustrating it was to watch myself plummet back into extreme levels of suffering. As usual, there was no particular cause to which I could ascribe my falling down a deep well into illness. The lack of an explanation was another element of my plight that added to my feelings of insanity.

My parents returned to town but even their presence could not change the level of pain I experienced each night. With their encouragement, I went to a local general practice doctor and explained what was happening. I gave him the list of anti-depressants I had tried at Harvard, all the medications that had made me ill and done my symptoms no good. Those drugs were mostly in the category called tricyclic anti-depressants. The doctor gave me a prescription for Zoloft, a common anti-depressant in a different category. Zoloft is one of what are known as "selective serotonin reuptake inhibitors" or SSRI drugs. I started it and immediately experienced headaches and nausea, common side effects of psych drugs. On the good side, it didn't make the psychiatric symptoms worse, as Prozac – the granddaddy of SSRI medications – had done at Harvard. But the side effects were quite significant.

The truth about SSRI medications – and many psych drugs – is that side effects kick in right away while any good effects the drugs may have only appear on the scene several weeks later. I was faithfully taking Zoloft each day, but my psychiatric symptoms continued to worsen. What I couldn't know was whether with more time the medication would help, or whether Zoloft would simply not be useful for me. Amid that uncertainly I was mostly impressed by one thing I knew clearly: my life was on the line, just as it had been at Harvard. When the exhaustion and suffering became fully excruciating, I tearfully begged my parents for help, shivering and shaking as I did so. We had to find something new, either a new treatment or perhaps a new doctor. We talked over what we knew of our options, and going to a psych ward in the hospital in Lewiston, Idaho, about an hour's drive from my home, seemed to be the best alternative. I had no insurance and I had no money, but the hospital was a Catholic one with a reputation for taking in ill people regardless of their ability to pay.

I was frightened about committing myself to a locked psychiatric unit in Idaho, an institution I knew might function quite differently from the sophisticated and well-funded general hospital in which I'd spent so much time at Harvard. But I also felt I had no choice but to try institutionalization. My parents drove me to the hospital and I checked in through the emergency room. I parted from my mother and father at the locked steel door on the fifth floor. Taking just two short steps I left my parents behind and entered the hospital environment, the heavy metal door locking shut behind me.

A nurse checked me into the psych unit, going through my basic medical history and what medications I had tried in the past. When she asked what I was feeling, I tried to describe the tortured images my mind was dreaming up and the physical exhaustion from which I was suffering. I trembled as I tried to express how frustrating it was to fall ill once more even when life and work were going well. At one point I said to the nurse I simply "felt like I was going to explode" as I fell into yet another abyss of suffering. For one reason or another, that phrase made it into the hospital notes.

After I got over the plunge of stepping into the locked ward, I took a small tour of the psychiatric facilities St. Joseph's Hospital had to offer. Across from the nurses' station were two important rooms. First was a large and pleasant space with windows on two sides that served as a dining room and a place for patients to hang out between meals. It was mostly full of tables and chairs, but along one of the interior walls it had a long counter and a fridge. There were crackers, peanut butter, and the like available on the counter 24/7, with milk and cheese in the refrigerator. A locked door of the room led to a small space that was used for craft projects. I would soon learn that the same staffer who took some of us upstairs to the exercise rooms in the mornings opened the craft room on certain afternoons and supervised our use of everything from colored pencils and papers printed with patterns for coloring to small kits of wooden pieces from which birdhouses could be glued together.

Next to the large room where we ate was a medium-sized space that had overstuffed chairs and a television. High on one wall was fastened a tear-off daily calendar. I noted that the calendar had not been updated for a couple of days, so it was announcing an incorrect day of the week and date to anyone who glanced at it. That fact might have been considered problematic, particularly in a psychiatric ward, where patients are sometimes asked the day of the week to test how connected they are with reality. But the calendar was too high for me to reach, so I didn't update it.

Stepping out of the TV room near the nurses' station, I came to a small space with a couple of vinyl-covered sofas. A battered and worn Reader's Digest was on a low table between the sofas. I picked it up but quickly set it aside, too upset to try to read even intellectually easy material. Then I walked a couple of times around the circular hallway that connected all the spaces of the psychiatric ward. The hallway began and ended at the nurses' station and dining room, giving me a tour of the doors that led to all the patients' rooms and a couple of interview rooms near the locked and heavy metal door that led out of the ward.

One special space on the interior side of the hallway was a room where basic medical exams were done on patients as they entered the ward. Weight and blood pressure were measured there, and a thorough search was made for drugs or items people might use to harm themselves. When I had been checked in, the nurse conducting the search on me had found foam earplugs in my pocket. The unusual items gave her pause, as she contemplated whether the plugs were contraband. I explained that I was at best a light sleeper, and noises awaken me, so I cram the plugs into my ears when I go to bed to block out at least soft sounds. In the end, the nurse decided I could keep the earplugs, and that simple decision on her part helped me rest at night throughout my stay in the hospital.

The ward's hallway allowed me to make a circuit of all the spaces that now defined my life. I did several laps around the hall, looping back to the nurses' station each time. As I walked around in circles I briefly tried to pray, but my mind was too confused to allow me to concentrate even on the Lord's prayer, a traditional set of verses I had learned by heart as a child. In the end all I could do was walk, putting one foot ahead of the other, with my mind racing along to a variety of ideas, including some linked to self-destruction.

My first night in the psych ward was a long one. I had a roommate, a woman who didn't speak to me so I didn't speak to her. At intervals, a nurse came into our room with a flashlight to check on us. Even with earplugs and lying on my side so my face was away from the intruding flashlight, I slept only a few hours and quite lightly. The next day I started to be incorporated into the rhythms of the ward. Breakfast arrived on a large and multi-tiered push cart and we patients ate it together. Then there was a group meeting, at which the ward rules were reviewed and simple group therapy was administered.

At some point that first day I spoke to one of the nurses. I explained I was concerned about being in the ward because I knew I couldn't pay my bill. I viewed that simple fact as a serious moral problem. On the one hand, I didn't want to accumulate a debt I knew I couldn't pay, but on the other hand, I had come to the hospital in an effort to save my life. I explained I was a church person and I asked if moral concerns were the type of thing a hospital chaplain might be able to help me sort out. The nurse said she'd let the chaplain's office know I would appreciate a chance to talk.

Soon enough, a middle-aged nun came to meet with me. She was the head of pastoral care of the hospital and had a simple but deep grace about her. I explained my difficulty. She assured me that not everyone treated in the hospital would be able to pay. She commended me for thinking about the matter in moral terms, but also pointed out the simple reality that if I were not well, I couldn't work and have any way of paying any bills at all. She urged me to concentrate on my treatment and let money and financial obligations sort themselves out later.

The nun spoke to me quite differently from the way the doctors and nurses did. The Sister seemed to feel we were colleagues on an equal footing, both engaged in the same work. It was a blessing simply to speak to her, and because she urged me not to torture myself with moral concerns on top of everything else, I tried to clear my mind and think only about what ailed me. The nun promised she'd check back with me in a day or two to see how I was doing. That simple act of decency encouraged me still more.

Days went by and I fell into the uncomplicated flow of psych ward life. I shot baskets in the exercise room, tried to eat something at each meal, and went to group meetings I greatly disliked. I continued to take increasing amounts of Zoloft and although I felt no good effects from the drug, I certainly experienced side-effects. Still, in the limbo known as institutionalization, side-effects were simply another thing to be endured.

Many psych drugs produce quite specific effects when a person first starts taking them. For me, Zoloft produces a very particular type of headache, high in the skull and sharp. To this day I recognize it, and I call it a "Zoloft headache" in the notes I keep for myself about how I'm faring. But if things go well when one takes a psych drug, the body gradually adapts to the medication and the intensity of the side effects decrease. When that occurs, it's time to increase the dosage of the medication, triggering the side effects all over again.

I managed to stay in touch with Sheldon Judson, my former Princeton teacher, during this difficult time. A telephone in the psych ward hung in the hall by the nurses' station. I called Sheldon collect, gave him the number, and he called me back. He encouraged me as best he could over the phone lines. If Zoloft failed to help, I told him, the doctors were discussing with me the possibility of going northward to Spokane for electro-convulsive therapy, as shock treatment is formally known. While ECT has evolved and improved over the years, it's still a treatment of last resort. But although I feared shock treatment, I couldn't argue with the fact that push was coming to shove yet again in my life, and all treatment avenues had to be explored. The love of my friends and family had not been enough to keep the rattlesnakes at bay, and Zoloft was doing no good. Sheldon listened to all I had to say, wishing me both luck and courage as I wrestled once more with the powerful demons that had shaped my life for most of my years.

After I had been in the psych ward a little more than a week the psychiatrist in charge of my case told me it was time for me to be discharged. I felt just as badly at that point as I had when I was admitted, so I put my head down and wept. At one level I understood the doctor's decision. I wasn't paying my bill and my bed might be needed for someone who either had private insurance or was at least a Medicaid patient. But more fundamentally, I felt I was being pushed out into the broader world well before I was ready for the challenge.

I had been in touch with my Quaker friends in Cambridge when things started to go south in my mind and again when I headed for the psych ward. When I got out of the hospital, a well-to-do Friend bought an airplane ticket so that my friend Cliff could come to visit me. Cliff had been a comrade as well as a Quaker mentor of mine when I was at Harvard. When he arrived in my rural Northwest home, I felt buoyed up. I was still desperately ill, but I could also count my obvious blessings and I knew I had been given several of them: my father, my mother, and Cliff, to name only the most obvious.

Cliff settled into the guest bedroom of my parents' house and we spent all our time together. We talked, and walked, and talked some more. I introduced Cliff to the clergyman at the nearby Episcopal church. The three of us talked, and walked together, helping me pass the time.

Quite unexpectedly, the day came when I finally had some glad tidings to report about my internal state. The news hinged on an experience I had while standing in the street in front of my parents' house where I had felt a clear, and good, effect of the Zoloft I had by then been taking for several weeks.

"I just felt a lot better. And I know it's from the drug," I said to my mother and Cliff. "It's gone now and I feel as terribly as ever, but I felt very different for a few minutes."

As the days after that unfolded, the good effects of Zoloft returned and became steadier. Thereafter, I made real progress. There was still a long road ahead of me until I was back on my feet, but the medication definitely was starting to help.

After getting out of the hospital I briefly was under the care of a psychiatrist who had come to my hometown from California. He didn't stay long – I suspect he simply didn't make money at the rate he was used to – but I was his patient while he was in town. He talked me into supplementing Zoloft with lithium, an old and basic mood stabilizer. I tried lithium for a few days, but the tremor it gave me was too terrible to bear. Thus, it was that with Zoloft alone in my bloodstream I picked up my life where I had left off and returned to work in the geology department.

The next few years were easier. Zoloft kept my suicidal thoughts at bay and made it possible for me to reliably work about half-time. I labored as a part-time instructor, teaching several different 100 and 200-level courses in the geology department. I also wound up a third and then a fourth and final murder mystery. Then, working with my colleague Larry, I started work on a second textbook. Although I was still crippled compared to what I termed the normal people around me, I was producing written work and meeting my daily obligations as a part-time teacher.

One of my friends from the Episcopal Church was a medical doctor who spoke to me one Sunday and asked how I was doing. I explained that insomnia was still my greatest enemy.

"Come down to the office and see me," he said. "I think I've got an anti-depressant that might help you sleep better."

I did as he encouraged and came away with a prescription for Remeron, an anti-depressant quite different from those in the SSRI group. Remeron is taken at night and, at least for me, it has the effect of calming the brain. Simply put, the medication truly helped me to sleep. Soon enough I looked forward to my nightly dose of the drug, and I reveled in getting more hours of sleep and in slumbering more deeply.

The transition to better sleep was stunning for a previously incurable insomniac like myself. Crawling into bed, turning out the light, and then actually falling asleep, all became fairly routine accomplishments. Weeks and then months passed under the dual influence of Zoloft and Remeron. With sleep under my belt each night and the anti-depressant effects of the two drugs, I had more energy to work during the day. My life began to blossom and I gave the new drug all the credit for that fact. Eight years had passed since I returned home, a staggering length of time in some respects, but at least I had made real progress and I seemed to have found medications that helped.

Under the influence of the two drugs now firmly woven into my life, I could finally change how I lived. I had repaid my undergraduate student loans during the time I lived in my parents' house, essentially using the advances on the murder mysteries for that obligation. With my parents' help, I got together a down payment and made an offer on a tiny, 700-square-foot house in our neighborhood. The one-bedroom house had a backyard the size of a postage stamp. But it was a home of my own, and I felt much more like an autonomous adult when I moved into it.

Having a place to call my own allowed me to act on one of my life's deepest loves – canine companionship. One of the mysteries of my heart is that I've always been deeply fond of dogs. As a preschooler, my favorite toy was a stuffed dog that I carried around until it disintegrated. My family eventually had three mongrels when I was a child, each of them acquired for my sake, not that of my brother or my parents.

True, at Princeton and Harvard I had been dogless. But that was because I had been both a serious student and a renter, two factors that argued against complicating my life with a dog. As soon as I started to establish an independent life back home, I wanted to add canines to my world. Perhaps it's no great surprise I love dogs so much. Unlike people, dogs are always happy to go for a walk with me – no matter the hour nor the weather – and they don't mind the crazy way I sometimes talk or the pauses I must take occasionally as I listen to what seems like encoded messages in common sounds.

When I decided to add dogs to my life, I was influenced by the highly witty English story of Dodie Smith about the hundred-and-one Dalmatians. Sane people might not acquire a high-energy breed because of a story book, but then mental stability has never been my strong suit. So it was I took the plunge and bought two Dalmatian puppies, one male and one female, from a backyard breeder north of Spokane, Washington.

The dogs were both a delight to me and the source of a great deal of daily work. I loved their playful energy, displayed almost 24-7. In some ways, from a simple management point of view, it was good there were two of them – they played with each other almost non-stop and sometimes, at least, managed to fatigue one another. When they were little, I took them for walks around the neighborhood, they were so cute they made people stop their yardwork to come speak with me. While I don't defend acquiring pure-bred dogs in a world full of unwanted strays in need of a home, and while all the dogs I've adopted since have come from the dog pound, I will always remember with delight the golden summer I had two rambunctious Dalmatian puppies tumbling over each other in their unquenchable exuberance.

With Remeron helping me to sleep, a tiny house of my own, and some good dogs, my life was blossoming. There was progress on other fronts, too. I went on a few dates with a couple of different men. We didn't click, and I didn't even consider going to bed with them. But it felt good at least to be back in circulation. I knew that if I were to marry and have children, I needed to find the right man soon.

But whenever I thought about children, I always came back to the idea that I was too unwell to bring babies into the world. My whole life had had so many episodes of deep illness, I didn't want to sign up to be a mother. It's one thing to do rather poorly at the job of being a wife, I reasoned, but having children, yet regularly being unavailable for the daily demands of motherhood, is quite a different story.
Perhaps because my mother had been so devoted to her children, I didn't want to be a poor mother due to illness. So, although I might still have had some daydreams of a family founded by Prince Charming

and me, they were only that – daydreams. I thought the world was surely better off without my having kids. And without children as part of the bargain, a long-term relationship with a man didn't look so rosy – at least not when I sized up the flesh-and-blood men I knew who were available. Such were my pragmatic thoughts about romance as I moved into my late 30s.

But while my dealings with men were rather marginal, nearly all other parts of my life were rich and expanding. I bought a vehicle for the first time in my life, a second-hand Chevy SUV large enough to tow a small, 25-year-old travel trailer I acquired. I went on some camping trips, and although it was stressful to sleep alone in the back-of-beyond, I successfully coped with the tensions and was glad for the sense of freedom the trailer gave me as I traveled. My dogs adapted well to camping, as dogs generally do, and my little trailer was a grand, if tiny, home away from home for us.

During this time, I did some work for the National Park Service, the branch of the government that administers the campgrounds around the 200-mile-long reservoir behind Grand Coulee Dam. The reservoir is known as Lake Roosevelt because Franklin Roosevelt was president when the mammoth dam was constructed. Camping out and wearing the "Smokey Bear" hat of the Park Service was a kick for me. My dogs enjoyed the freedom to romp along the shores of the lake or run across the fields and through the woods of the land nearby.

On hot days, even the Dalmatian who hated water strode into the reservoir up to her shoulders. On torrid days, I did the same. Then, while cruising one afternoon on a Park Service boat, I saw some outcrops along the reservoir's edge that intrigued me as a geologist. When time permitted, I borrowed a motorboat from family friends at home and towed it to Lake Roosevelt. I started to do research on the unusual outcrops that made up the reservoir's bluffs during my free time, taking photos and notes of the striking sand and mud beds they contained. Soon I was convinced the outcrops recorded more than one story of catastrophic flooding in the late Ice Age.

Geologists are in agreement that there were massive floods across the inland Northwest that came from an enormous lake in what's now western Montana. Glacial Lake Missoula, as the ancient body of water is known, was held in place by a dam of ice. In its day, Lake Missoula was as large as Lake Superior is today. In the late Ice Age, the crucial ice dam either collapsed or floated off the rock that lay beneath it. Immediately, the waters of Lake Missoula poured westward. Very quickly, a whole region was inundated by violent floodwaters. The event shaped the surface of the region, carving enormous gashes in the earth like Grand Coulee and laying down huge gravel bars.

Part of the floodwaters from Lake Missoula came down the Spokane River, where I found evidence of the inundation. Getting around by motorboat rather than by truck, I quickly inspected all the bluffs that lined the shores of Lake Roosevelt. I documented flood evidence and took samples of the sand and gravel beds left behind by the waters of Lake Missoula. Next, just to be thorough, I started up the arm of Lake Roosevelt made by the Columbia River. The Columbia flows south from British Columbia into Washington State, joining the Spokane River valley at a confluence where I was camping. To my delight, I found evidence up the Columbia that another major flood had inundated the area from the north. I took samples and photographed features of what I hypothesized was a different but equally enormous catastrophic flood arriving into my part of Washington from Canada.

My time working along the shores of Lake Roosevelt was good, but it was marked by one personal blow. Back in my hometown that spring I had become involved with a faculty member in another science department at the university. Mark was a bit older than I, but with a quick mind that made it fun to spend time with him. I hadn't been in a sexual relationship for a long time, and I was glad to find a man with whom I initially seemed to be a match. But that summer Mark abruptly gave me a box of European chocolates and unilaterally broke off our involvement. I felt deep grief, as well as the bitter sting of rejection. My intensity and high energy levels, I came to suspect, had driven away someone with whom I wanted to continue to be involved. But after a few days of tears, I had to move forward from what had really only been a brief affair and return to serious work along the shores of Lake Roosevelt.

In other ways, the summer spent doing field geology was good. Using the early work as a springboard, I applied for a one-semester sabbatical from my university, offering to investigate the Ice Age sediments still more. I was granted the sabbatical leave. In the summer of 2001, I worked once more for the Park Service at Lake Roosevelt. When fall began I simply kept my travel trailer where it was and, using the borrowed motorboat, went to work full time researching what Mother Nature could tell me about catastrophic floods that had swept down through the region from two different directions as the last Ice Age waned.

That fall was marked by many internal highs, as I stumbled around looking at outcrops and marveling at the complexity of what I was seeing. I didn't know the explanation for everything I saw, but I learned each day directly from nature. In the evenings I studied the books and papers I had back in my trailer, my dogs resting at my feet. It was an exhilarating time, intense and pure, like some of the early days of being a graduate student at Harvard before the illness came to dominate my time there. But although I felt good and enjoyed my work, I didn't have mystical or other truly extreme experiences. I was simply a woman deeply in love with what she was doing, eager to learn from Mother Nature as much as I could about a dramatic chapter of geologic history.

There were times I felt the stress of working alone in a thoroughly rural area. I knew that if I broke my ankle, I would be the only person I could call on to somehow get back to a road or a place where others could potentially help me. I wondered idly what would happen if I met a man out in the boondocks who was intent on harming me. But the romance of the work more than made up for the stress I sometimes felt about being alone. The weather was gorgeous that fall and I enjoyed it, the work, the dogs, and communing with geologic evidence all day, every day.

Because I was camping, I nearly missed the events of September 11th,

2001, learning only late in the day and by chance of the attacks in New York and at the Pentagon. Stupefied by what my vehicle's radio seemed to be reporting about the World Trade Center, I went to a Ranger Station to talk to someone about what had happened. The rangers confirmed the almost incredible news. Overcome with emotion, I quit work for the day and went back to where my travel trailer stood. I spent an hour in my vehicle with the engine off, just listening to National Public Radio and its coverage of the attacks.

Immersed in nature, as I had been, it was easy to be even more thoroughly disoriented by that day's news than if I had been back home in the work-a-day world. But the events of the 11th didn't send me into a tailspin. I recovered a sense of equilibrium as the days following the attacks unfolded, and I carried on with the field research. As the fall progressed, I worked hard, scouring more and more of the outcrops along the shores of Lake Roosevelt. I stayed at my campsite until the start of November. When it snowed on All Saints Day, I decided to break camp and head for home where I could busy myself indoors by starting some laboratory work on my samples. I left my campsite feeling cold and tired, but glad for my time at Lake Roosevelt.

My sabbatical leave, though brief, had been a good one for me. When it came to an end I returned to teaching with a rejuvenated spirit. But soon I was looking for something more to do than just my part-time teaching gig at the university. I talked to the chairman of the geology department, essentially asking for more work and a larger number of teaching assignments. He said he didn't have money to hire me full-time, so I started to look around for other work I might be able to pick up.

When the local newspaper advertised for a part-time reporter, I gladly answered the ad. I met with the managing editor and explained that although I had no background or education in journalism, I was a quick study and would do everything I could to be useful to the paper. To my surprise he hired me on a half-time basis. I'd be working at just a fraction more than the minimum wage, but I'd be learning a new trade, and the challenge of coming up to speed in quite a new arena appealed to me. Thus, I plunged into the project of learning how to be a small-town reporter feeding stories into the voracious maw that is a daily newspaper.

My first lesson in the newspaper biz was that I wasn't writing for The New York Times. The editors wanted short pieces with quotations sprinkled liberally throughout the stories. My beat was the smaller towns around the area covered by the paper – truly tiny towns, some with populations numbering only in the hundreds. It was an interesting job, one in which I found myself writing about alpacas and the people who raised them, wood carvings and those who made them, and a three-thousand-year-old cedar tree standing near where the last road ended in the mountains of Idaho. I grew into the job, learned a lot, and had fun along the way.

More than once, I thanked the good Lord my medical friend from church had thought to give me a bottle of Remeron. My sabbatical and the new adventures at work were all made possible only by that drug, I was sure. It's interesting to think you owe the contours of your life to a medication originally given to you largely by chance, but I simply accepted my good fortune.

Although my life was better than it had been for many years, it was still far from easy. I had times of excess energy, and blasts of power that made it hard to sit still during the day or triggered explosions of rapid thinking. I walked for miles and miles indeed, I did so almost on a daily basis. The habit delighted my dogs, who always came with me. But my compulsion to walk wore out even sturdy shoes. To try to simultaneously lick my high-energy states and help my joints, I started to swim once again. The swimming felt good but only sometimes did it help to tire me. It was disconcerting to admit it, but even an hour-long swim could barely slow me down when my energy levels were high.

Throughout this period, I continued to live under the diagnosis of recurrent, major depression. That understanding of what ailed me was never entirely satisfactory. It ignored my high-energy states, including those extreme enough they caused me real suffering. And since I had not admitted my auditory symptoms to the doctors, they were not part of my diagnosis. My failure to speak up may seem distinctly odd on my part, but I was in denial even with myself about the maniacal laughter and the messages in common sounds I sometimes heard. So, when the doctors said I was depressed, I at least largely trusted the diagnosis. Of course, I had been marginally helped by Zoloft and significantly helped by Remeron, two anti-depressant drugs. That seemed to affirm the diagnosis of depression. From my perspective now I was awfully naïve at that stage of life. But hindsight is always clearer than foresight, and all I can say about that time was that I did what I could to understand my situation.

CHAPTER 5:

PROGRESSION OF THE DISORDER

I've not been a person to stick with the same job too long. I'm not particularly proud of it, but I've changed jobs several times since returning to my hometown, including when I certainly didn't need to. After years working as an instructor in the geology department at Washington State University, my wanderlust and my impatience got the better of me. I was frustrated with many of the other faculty in the department, a collection of men who could agree things were going downhill but could never come together on how to address our group's decline. After one too many faculty meetings in which all suggestions for change were shot down but no alternatives were offered, I started to look for other work.

As it happened, the local newspaper for which I'd been a part-time reporter was advertising for a full-time person. I applied and was offered the job. The pay was low – a tradition in the newspaper realm and always the case at small papers. But setting aside the pay, there were a couple of things I really liked about the work. I value the community in which I live – I have watched the institutions in my hometown grow and develop over the decades. I know many people from different walks of life throughout the community, some I've known since childhood. So, after giving the matter about one minute's consideration, I accepted the newspaper job, resigned from my university position, and plunged ahead.

Filling a daily newspaper with materials a small staff generates is a challenge. The boss explained to me that my quota of stories was a minimum of six per week – one for each of the six days, Monday through Saturday, the paper came out. He also said I could have two weeks to explore my beat and talk with people, but then the quota would need to be filled. Sobered more than a bit by the number of pieces I would need to produce, I jumped into my job, hoping I could quickly learn to swim.

My official beat was everything in the county connected to education: the schools, a small branch of a community college, and the large state university where I had taught. I made the rounds, introducing myself to the administrators of the various educational institutions. One thing I felt strongly about was that the paper had tended to neglect the area's private K-12 schools. There is a small Catholic grade school in an outlying hamlet of my county and there are two evangelical Christian schools in my hometown of Pullman. Some of the first stories I did were about those three schools, trying to introduce my readers to their characters and strengths, as well as what was happening in them.

Although my official beat was education, as I grew into my job, I covered a wide variety of things. When the situation demanded it, I reported on murder and rape trials, fires, city council meetings, an emergency landing at the local airport, and all sorts of other topics. In short, I did what the paper needed each day.

I loved doing the work. It appealed to the idealism in me. I genuinely felt good about producing responsible coverage of local issues, and thus, I hoped, to help the community I value so deeply. At the same time, some of my story topics were stressful and required personal growth. Covering child rape was probably the toughest type of story I did. Going to court and hearing the evidence was itself intense, but trying to strike up conversations during breaks with friends and relatives of the defendant – or with the defendant himself – was a formidable challenge given how strongly my stomach was sometimes churning. Talking with the victim's family was no less draining. It took everything I had in me to cover those trials.

I dreamt up an additional task beyond reporting while working at the newspaper. I thought it could be fun to write a column about the local geology of the area. The paper's editors were not convinced such a piece would get wide interest, but since it cost them nothing to have me try my hand at the work, they let me go ahead with the column as an experiment. I wrote about topics like the nearby localities to dig garnets or unearth fossils, or the geologic history of the area and how that history had led to the landscape in which we were living. The pieces found an audience. I called the column "The Rock Doc" and, I liked to think, I got better at doing it as I went along.

My natural intensity worked in my favor in the journalism realm. Newspaper reporters and editors are an intense lot, used to producing lots of work that meets frequent deadlines. From my point of view, the daily deadline was in some ways a pleasure. If I turned out six stories per week, I knew I was keeping up with what was expected of me. Unlike faculty work, where larger goals and responsibilities are less clearly defined, being a reporter was much more black-and-white. There was also the pleasure of meeting tight deadlines and seeing my work in print each day. Every writer craves readers, and as a reporter, I had readers each day. It was tough not to love what I was doing.

There was one fly in the ointment, however. Small newspapers pay their staff a pittance. I would have had trouble making ends meet on the work I did for the paper alone. Happily, I shopped myself around to several textbook publishers and found one that needed a freelance editor for freshmen geology and oceanography textbooks. Off-and-on I worked on projects for the company, often staying late at the paper to get in a little time on my freelance job or coming in on weekends to accomplish the same task. It wasn't easy working seven days per week, of course, but the freelance work paid well and I needed the money, so I was truly glad for it. The work also kept me thinking a bit about teaching and the basics of freshman science. Overall, I was lucky to have the work, and I enjoyed cranking out web-based materials for the publisher or editing the next textbook edition.

I worked at the newspaper for three years, piling up about 1,000 stories under my by-line. But eventually, when I simply was tired of the meager salary I earned at the paper, I took advantage of an opportunity to go back to the faculty at the university.

One day I was on campus to interview an associate dean of science. She explained that she had hired one person to teach new, interdisciplinary science classes at the freshman level, and she was looking for another. I was all ears and said I would be happy to be hired for that job, doubly so because I knew the first hire, a woman trained in entomology, and, as it happened, a person with whom I had grown up.

But before I could jump into the new job, I had another round of illness to endure. In my last spring at the newspaper, I decided to use my vacation days for a long camping trip. Towing the same 1972 travel trailer I had used for sabbatical, I drove south to Nevada to visit a geologist friend from graduate school. Elizabeth was working at the Round Mountain gold mine at the time, and I arrived at the small mining camp with my faithful dog and the trailer towed by my Chevy Blazer.

The early phases of that trip seemed stressful, but they had at least some delight woven into them. I was glad to be camping once more, and eager to explore Nevada for the first time. For a geologist, a place like Nevada is wonderful because the rocks are exposed, not buried under many feet of soil. With maps and books beside me, I drove through the Nevada desert, marveling at the geologic record laid out around me in the rocks of the region. I was feeling too intense for comfort, I knew, but travel and poor sleep in the travel trailer could both easily contribute to my feeling frazzled.

After I reached Round Mountain, Elizabeth and her husband took me off into the desert to visit a historic mine site one day, and then the following day we toured the enormous open-pit mine at Round Mountain itself. The highlight of the tour was hearing the noon whistle blow and seeing the detonations go off on the floor of the great pit. The earth shook and dust rose from the blast as we peered over into the pit from its rim. Very kindly, Elizabeth gave me three gold nuggets that employees of the mine were allowed to purchase. I still treasure them as keepsakes.

But I wasn't well, and as the trip progressed, I had to admit that more clearly to myself. I slept little and, as always, the greater the trouble I had with insomnia the more hellish was my mental state. I felt the presence of my personal rattlesnakes on the ground around me. In

Nevada, real rattlers are a possibility, a fact that complicated my response to the mental snakes that have tormented me for so long.

In addition to mental problems, I had some simple bad luck with my vehicle. Driving on the gravel roads of rural Nevada took its toll on my tires. One fine day, a tire blew out. I knew I might be in trouble when Elizabeth, looking my vehicle over, said, "Do you only have one spare?"

Although I thought my mid-sized Chevy SUV used pretty standard tires, in rural Nevada my tires were considered small and unusual. Everyone else, it seemed, drove a full-sized pickup. When my first tire blew, the weight of the vehicle bent the rim before I could fully stop. A kindly local man tried to hammer it back into the round by hand, but it was clearly substandard from that point onward. Elizabeth helped me get into a larger town where I could buy the one new tire that was available in my size. Thus, I again had one spare, but on a bad rim. When a second tire on my SUV blew, it was clear to me that the next two tires could go at any time – and I had nothing to replace them.

The stress I felt about the blowouts and the difficulty of obtaining new tires started to mount within me. I felt isolated in rural Nevada, running the risk that the next mile of driving would fully cripple my humble little outfit. When I left Elizabeth and Round Mountain, my highest priority was to get to a city and buy new tires. I drove carefully on paved highways, across central Nevada and into Utah. Finally, I arrived at a town large enough to have a full-scale tire store. I had two new tires put on the vehicle and bought a new spare tire and rim. While I was relieved to have the tires, I was also alarmed at the intensity of the distress I had felt about them. I was all wound up emotionally, and I had to admit as I sat in the tire store waiting for the work to be done that the tire blow outs were simply the occasion for giving me something specific to obsess about.

But it wasn't clear what I could do about my mental health. Many is the time I have felt unwell and soldiered on. Sometimes, things start to go better for no apparent reason I can discern. One thing was clear: I was many hundreds of miles from home, so I knew I couldn't get back to my house quickly no matter what I decided to do. Confused by my distress, and likely not thinking clearly, I hoped the new tires would change my luck and help me relax into something more nearly approximating normal mental states.

Looking back, I should have recognized the danger I was running and pointed my Chevy for home when I left the tire store. But there was one more place I had planned to go on the trip, a spot in southern Utah about which I'd read for a number of years and that I was curious to see. Best Friends Animal Sanctuary is an enormous animal shelter in the Utah desert, a place that's home – either temporarily or permanently – for hundreds of dogs, cats, horses, rabbits, mules, and much more. As a dog-lover, I had read about this mother-of-all animal shelters in the desert. I also had recently had to put down a Dalmatian dog of mine who had developed a malignancy in her old age. I still had one dog, a mutt named Buster Brown, originally adopted from a local dog pound, but I was interested in acquiring a second canine companion. So, with my new tires I pointed my vehicle and travel trailer south – away from my home – and drove to the town of Kanab, Utah.

I arrived in Kanab in the early evening. I was pretty wound up and didn't sleep much at all that night. I tried to talk myself out of my distress, but my surging adrenalin levels don't level off simply because of the sermons I give myself. Still, I got what rest I could and, in the morning, Buster Brown and I made our way to Best Friends. It's an impressive facility, a small city of animals and the people who care for them. I wandered among the dog pens, which were numerous and full of cheerfully barking dogs, and then I stopped by the headquarters building to ask about adoption.

When I mentioned to a staffer that I'd had Dalmatians, he called up the record of what Dalmatians were on hand at the moment at Best Friends. There were a couple of pure-bred Dalmatians, but they were senior citizens and I was interested in a younger animal. A Dalmatian-hound mix about 1 year old seemed potentially to fit the bill. I then met the dog. He intrigued me, perhaps because although he looked a lot like a Dalmatian, he bayed like a hound. Although I've had various types of dogs over the years, I'd never had a hound to call my own, and I thought Mulligan Stew was a sufficiently interesting canine mix I should try adopting him. I introduced Mulligan to Buster Brown. They sniffed each other tentatively but peacefully and both seemed to accept that the other existed on the planet.

Suddenly, as I stood there with the two dogs at my feet, I felt an enormous surge of adrenalin. In an instant, I was in the throes of a full-blown panic attack. I struggled to breathe as calmly as I could, and to talk myself through the wave of fear that engulfed me. Only the fact that I have years – nay, decades – of practice dealing with unusual mental states prevented me from running screaming across the parking lot. But even I was hard pressed to remain outwardly calm.

But busy as I was with my own bodily problems, I also felt I had to make some decision about Mulligan Stew. I was at Best Friends, which was likely a once-in-a-lifetime experience. I had interviewed a potential new dog, and the time had come to say Yea or Nay to him. Stressed though I was, I was also irrationally hopeful, perhaps because of the spirit of my visit to Best Friends. I opted to adopt. When I put Mulligan and Buster into the back of my vehicle, there was some canine tension, but no fight broke out, and I seemed to calm down just a bit at the sight of the pair of dogs safely ensconced in my vehicle.

I filled out the paperwork at Best Friends and paid my adoption fee. Then I finally pointed my Chevy and the aged travel trailer north, toward home. It was afternoon when I started the journey I planned to do over about three days. I drove north through southern Utah that first day. When I camped in the evening, I was alarmed to find my sense of intensity and distress was rapidly mounting, not dropping. Objectively speaking, nothing was wrong, but that didn't seem to matter. I took tranquilizers, but despite them I slept very little. For their part, the two dogs didn't sleep deeply on the floor of the travel trailer – they had a lot of emotional adjustment to go through before they would feel comfortable with each other.

Dawn of the next day found me exhausted and still a very long way from home. Still, there was nothing I could see to do except drive north. I did so, knowing that my level of fatigue was swiftly reaching the point that I wasn't a good driver. Tormented by my internal distress and simultaneously by how deeply tired I had so rapidly become, I drove as much as I could, taking frequent stops to keep myself alert and give the nervous dogs the rest stops they enjoyed. In the evening I stopped south of Salt Lake City. I was utterly spent, tired of driving, of towing a travel trailer, of dealing with stressed-out dogs, and mostly tired of how absolutely wretched I felt. I thought to help myself by getting off the road early and taking the dogs on a very long walk around the town. We walked at first on city sidewalks, up one street and down another at random. After doing that for several miles, we walked to the edge of the town and then out into the desert, where the dogs could be off-leash.

The walking seemed to help me to slow down and relax a little bit, but I was still feeling deeply distressed. More than once that evening I had walked past the Latter-Day Saints Church. I knew there were good Mormons in the town, and I yearned to have a simple reassuring word from some church person. I felt that a small bit of encouragement might go a long way in helping me to calm my adrenalin-filled brain. But I'm not a Mormon, and it seemed unlikely that I could find some stranger who would say a reassuring thing that would help my tortured mind. Instead, I tried to breathe deeply and slowly in rhythm with my steps. While walking and throughout the evening in my trailer, I used the rational part of my brain to parade out each reassuring thought I could find rattling around in my tired head. Again and again, I told myself three good things like I had earlier in life, trying to reassure myself that I was okay.

But that night in the trailer everything got worse. Instead of finding some much-needed rest, I was tormented by panic flooding my bloodstream, more energy and alarm than anything I had felt on the trip. Soon I was shaking from head to toe, just as I had during my Harvard years. I took tranquilizers but they did nothing for me. Not only could I not sleep, I could not even lie still and pretend to rest. Within just a couple of hours I was a full basket case, maddened by the adrenalin and the stupefying levels of exhaustion in which I was immersed.

I couldn't make sense of what was wrong – but I did feel it was different from the worst days I'd known at Princeton and Harvard. There I had been laid low by illness, falling into a great pit of distress that felt quite different from what was wrong now. When I was ill as a student, I hated myself and contemplated suicide. That wasn't what was happening to me in Utah. I was harassed to the point of madness by illness, but it wasn't what I'd learned to call "depression." Over and over in my fevered mind, I went through how and why my present malady differed from what I'd known in the past. But, of course, in the end, none of that mattered. What was important was identifying what I could do to help myself, and on that important subject, I couldn't think of any useful palliative for what was so very wrong.

Finally, I got up and dug out my cell phone to see if I could pick up a signal with it. As luck would have it, there was good signal strength, something that can't be taken for granted in the rural West. But studying the face of my cell phone, I wasn't sure whom to call in the small hours of the morning – or what I should ask if I could reach someone. In the end, I dialed my brother's number. Sleepily, he answered. I tried to explain both where I was and what was wrong. I hadn't had a useful night's sleep for a number of days, I said, and the adrenalin levels were fully out of hand. I wouldn't be able to sleep enough to drive, I told him, certainly not drive the day and a half that still remained in my trip.

My brother put his wife on the phone. My sister-in-law works as a disability counselor, and she listened sympathetically to my tale of woe. Then she made what was to me a startling offer. She said she could fly the next day to the Salt Lake City airport. If I could meet her there, she could help drive my vehicle and the trailer home.

I blessed Krista's name and her good heart. I wasn't far south of Salt Lake, and with a specific plan like what she suggested, I began to see a way forward out of my predicament. I thanked her and said I would get myself and the dogs to the Salt Lake airport in the morning. She said she would call me back the next day when she knew her plane's schedule.

Once I got off the phone, I felt a good measure calmer. To be sure, I was still full of adrenalin and exhaustion, and there were mental rattlesnakes on the floor of the trailer – crowded though the floor was already with the two dogs. But with another round of tranquilizers and reassurance that my sister-in-law would be on her way, I napped until dawn. In the morning I towed the travel trailer up to Salt Lake. I studied the map of Utah I had in the car and successfully drove to the airport. The dogs and I arrived before my sister-in-law's flight. I walked the pooches around the parking lot, then lay down in the travel trailer with them to wait. I got the briefest of naps and felt better than I had for days. Krista called me when she arrived at the airport and I gave her directions to where my vehicle and the trailer were parked. She found us, hugged me, and didn't reproach me for wearing myself out to the point I required being rescued.

We drove north for the remainder of the day, reaching Boise by nightfall. Krista stayed in a motel room while the dogs and I stayed in my trailer. On the next day, we drove the rest of the way home. I was grateful to my sister-in-law and embarrassed about the trouble I had caused. Still, if she hadn't flown to Salt Lake, I'm not sure how I would have gotten my vehicle, the dogs, and the trailer home. When even repeated doses of tranquilizers cannot ease me into sleep, full disability is just a step away.

But while being home decreased the stress I felt, I was far from well. I settled into my little house again, but I continued having major problems sleeping. Soon it became clear to me it wasn't just adrenalin that was my enemy. Often at night, as I lay tossing and turning in bed, I'd be overwhelmed by the feeling of intense internal heat. I would be sweating all over and throwing off the bedding that covered me in just a moment. In short, I was suffering from my usual mental problems combined with a bad case of hot flashes and night sweats.

This new stage of life was an emotional turning point as well as a physical one. Nothing like the sudden onset of menopause can make it clearer that a woman is past her prime. Long before this time, I had decided I didn't want to bring children into the world. I was simply too ill, too often, I had reasoned, to take on child rearing responsibilities. That, in turn, had influenced and likely limited the amount of time and energy I was willing to put into finding a husband. But when I was younger and was making those decisions, it all felt voluntary. Now, in early middle age, outcomes were being taken away from me without my choice or input as a consideration. My body had unilaterally declared me over the hill, unable now to have a child. That fact didn't by any means knock me off my feet, but at some deep level, I quietly mourned the elimination of one branch of life experience I was never to explore.

I didn't have too much time to grieve, however, as I was busy finishing up one job and trying to deal with illness. It took time, but ultimately, I found a doctor willing to give me estrogen. That helped make the hot flashes manageable. But the adrenalin surges continued to be a problem. I was wretched, and I was losing weight at a brisk clip. My doctor measured the amount of adrenalin I produced over a 24-hour interval. The value was off the charts. That result, he explained, meant I might well have an adrenalin-secreting tumor somewhere in my body. The doctor explained I very much needed to see an endocrinologist in a medical facility adequate to hunt for such growth within me.

Because I felt wretched in a different way than I had at Harvard, I took the medical recommendation seriously. To be sure, I was having mental problems, but there also seemed to be something else at work. I knew nothing about adrenalin-secreting tumors, but the place to be evaluated for them was in a hospital in Seattle. Soon I had an appointment with an endocrinologist there. Because I was so very ill, I asked my mother if she would come with me. As always, she stepped up to the plate for me.

The trip to Seattle proved as pointless as it was expensive. While I was there my adrenalin levels were not terribly abnormal. Beyond that, the sophisticated scans and tests at the hospital couldn't detect any tumors in me. That was good news, of course, but it left what had happened to me in the spring and early summer as quite a mystery.

But that analysis lay in the distant future. When I came home from Seattle, all I knew was that I was unwell and apparently didn't have adrenalin-secreting tumors. I talked to my doctor about what continued to be wrong with me. I also talked to my friends about the predicament I was in. A wise and thoughtful friend recommended I see her psychiatrist in Lewiston, Idaho, the city about an hour's drive to the south of my hometown. I needed help, I knew, and although the psychiatrists at Harvard had never done anything useful for me, I was not above trying out the specialty one more time.

Even in the world of managed care and complex insurance regulations, initial visits to psychiatrists run for a full hour. Thus, I met for an hour with a tall and aging male psychiatrist who listened intently to what I had to say. I explained my long-term problems as best I could, mentioning the years at Harvard as having been the worst of my life and my repeated hospitalizations there. I referred to my problems as "depression" because that was the language I had been taught in which to discuss them. I explained that one anti-depressant medication had been a real help to me, helping limit my tendency toward suicidal thinking. A second anti-depressant allowed me to work full-time rather than part-time. But clearly, I was deeply ill again so, if my problems stemmed from mental health issues, my usual drugs were not up to the task of keeping me functional.

The doctor listened to all I had to say, asking a few questions as the conversation unfolded. In the end, he said I should come back for another appointment and try gabapentin to see if it would help me slow down and perhaps sleep a bit more. I filled his prescription and soon found that gabapentin was useful, both as an anti-anxiety agent and, when taken at night, as a drug that increased my chance of sleeping. I liked the new medication quite a bit. I didn't feel it hit my bloodstream, nor leave when it was spent. Instead, I simply felt calmer and better. With gabapentin, continued estrogen to control hot flashes, and the passage of a bit more time, I started to feel more like I had before the ill-fated camping trip. Soon I was regaining the weight and the strength I had lost when life had been so difficult.

My improvement could not have come at a better time because I was about to start a new and demanding job. I'd been hired back by the university not to teach geology courses, but interdisciplinary science classes. Working closely with the entomologist named Lisa, I was to co-teach introductory interdisciplinary science at both the regular and the honors levels. The job was a kick because Lisa and I had a blank slate on which to write. With full freedom about how to develop the courses, we threw ourselves into the work. Our goal was not to teach a number of facts about the natural world, but to show the students how science worked and how scientists make progress in research projects. The course spanned everything from the life and work of Charles Darwin to evidence for ancient and modern climate change. I've never been as happy teaching as I was in that job nor, I suspect, had I ever done work as good as I did with Lisa.

The climate change material really grabbed my attention as we taught the students about it. Climate change is not a new concept to geologists – we began to recognize clear signs of the Ice Age as long ago as the 1830s. For my part, I was happy to dig into the scientific literature about climate, including the strong evidence about natural climate change that has happened over long spans and also sometimes in terribly short periods, like a single human generation. The more I read about global temperature and precipitation patterns, the more interested I became. Soon I started writing a book about the matter, not a textbook but rather a book that an ordinary citizen might read. I studied climate, wrote about it, and studied some more. Many mornings I found the energy to get up at 5 a.m. so that I could read and write before going to work. Happily, I didn't become manic despite long days, I simply forged ahead on the climate project.

As the months ticked by, I came to strongly believe that the public discussion of climate in this country had become highly skewed, dominated as it was by what I'd term noisy alarmists on the one hand and intractable doubters on the other. To me, the technical evidence clearly suggests we are changing climate due to greenhouse gas emissions. But it's also true that climate would be changing on its own even if we humans had never existed. Those natural evolutions include substantial changes that sometimes play out in as little as 20 years. Finally, it's a basic fact that if temperatures were to drop rather than climb, we would be in a heap of trouble. Agriculture, especially in the U.S., Canada, Europe, Ukraine, and Russia would be crippled if a sharp drop in temperature occurs – a drop exactly like we've seen in the record of natural climate change in recent millennia. In short, I came to believe that unless we can discuss natural as well as man-made climate change, we will not be able to create useful climate and energy policies.

Life went on and, in the new teaching gig, one semester followed another. I occasionally kept appointments with the psychiatrist, but I had nothing major to report to him. Sometimes I took gabapentin fairly often, but then for weeks, I wouldn't take it at all. Life was about as good as it gets for me. There were, of course, mental rattlesnakes on the floor at times, but I was well familiar with their ways and I tolerated them. From time-to-time ordinary sounds were magnified and I heard messages in them, but I was used to such events and I ignored them as best I could. As long as I could sleep, the suffering in my mind didn't get out of control.

I did have some new problems with my physical health. I moved from one house to another one summer and, in the midst of all the work that moving entailed, both my knees started to absolutely burn with pain. The problem, it turned out, was bone-to-bone contact between my kneecaps and the weight-bearing bones of the knee joint. It seemed my decades of compulsive walking had caught up with me, wearing out the smooth material that should help those bones glide past one another. The pain varied at first from substantial to extreme. I could no longer do heavy work of any kind, not yard work or even heavy housework that required kneeling or deep bending of the knees.

During the worst phase with my knees, when I was on canes and hardly able to get from my car to my desk at work, I got a handicapped parking permit. At first, it was a temporary one, but when it expired and I was still in miserable shape, the doctor made it permanent. A couple of times I used the electric carts for the handicapped at the grocery store. I was glad for this kind of assistance but frustrated that I needed the help.

I didn't adapt to my new limitations without considerable grumbling. Again and again, I overdid it, throwing myself into some Saturday project in my house or doing something like leaf-raking, lawn mowing or snow shoveling. Whenever I did such work – even for a brief time – I experienced crippling pain in both knees. I had to use two canes to help myself get around for a time. That was a real workout for my arms and I could feel the stress in my shoulders. In short, I had a new health problem of major dimensions to manage. In time I accepted my fate and started to fully change the way I lived. Although I didn't like to do it, I hired a man to mow my lawn in the summer and plow my driveway in the winter. Gradually, the pain decreased as I "babied" my knees and took powerful anti-inflammatory drugs. I was able to put the canes in my closet and enjoy the simple freedom of walking normally once again.

There were some other major changes in my life as well. My parents had passed their 80th birthdays and their health was in decline. My father had both dementia and a neurological problem that made it increasingly difficult for him to stand and walk. When he fell at home, something he did with increasing frequency, my mother could not get him up again. At first, I could manage the trick, but as my father's strength continued to decay, I couldn't lift his deadweight to a position from which he could stand.

My mother had cared for my father for many years in their 70s, including as he went through three rounds of major surgery to replace both his knees and one shoulder. But she was old and ill herself, and she had reached the point at age 80 that she could not care for him. The day came when my brother and I moved my father into an assisted living facility so that I could take my mother to the hospital for a knee replacement of her own. That surgery went well, but it was clear to me my mother needed more help than we had been giving her. She was having trouble paying bills on time and I wasn't at all sure she was cooking well for herself. So, I bought a larger house to replace my tiny one, and moved her into my house to help supply the daily care she needed and to free up my parents' condominium so that it could be rented to help with my father's expenses.

Although it wasn't easy to deal with some of the work involved in caring for elderly parents, I was happy to do my part. My father and mother had always been extraordinarily generous with me, helping me survive my mental problems from my childhood until they were too old to help me anymore. It was clear to me that, to the extent possible, I should help them in their old age. My mother and I got along in my house pretty well, and on our good days, we shared laughter as well as conversation in the evenings. My dogs were glad to have her as company during the day when I was at work, and she came to enjoy the companionship the canines provided.

In terms of working life, my stint doing interdisciplinary science teaching had been a joy. But I have a thirst for new adventures and challenges, a feature of my being that may reflect part of my mental illness. In any case, when a new job at the university became available, I was happy enough to fill it.

It happened that the public relations director for WSU's College of Science had been stricken by a sudden stroke. She collapsed on the job, never to recover sufficiently to work again. The Dean of Science knew me, and knew I had worked for three years at the local newspaper. He asked whether I would be interested in working in PR rather than as a classroom teacher. After giving the matter a minute's consideration, I agreed to the plan. I figured I would learn more in the new job than I would be continuing as a classroom instructor. Once I made the switch the Dean announced he would be giving me an assistant to help me in my new role. Susan had been a staffer in the molecular biosciences department, but the Dean was going to move her to work under me. My instructions were to do whatever should be done to keep the college alumni informed about the good work being done in teaching and research.

Every day of the new role was interesting because I was new to PR and thus was learning a great deal. I sat in on a course in public relations offered by the communications department, hoping to learn what I could from it and improve on what I might be able to accomplish for the Dean. But mostly, I learned on the job. I profiled students, faculty, and alumni members. At first, Susan and I concentrated on print media, putting out hardcopy newsletters for a department and for the College as a whole.

In some ways being a PR agent was like being a reporter, but the stories on which I concentrated were always positive news, with no child rape or murder cases that had to be covered. Still, there were some emotional moments in the work. One undergraduate I interviewed broke down in the middle of our session together because her father had recently died and therefore wouldn't see her graduate, and another wept openly when discussing the death of a friend. In short, doing personal interviews with young people had emotional intensity, even within the framework of public relations.

My learning curve grew sharply steeper when I moved from print-based communication efforts to those of video and internet-based work. A videographer and I met with people I interviewed while she filmed. Then the videographer made the recordings into useful short pieces. It was a new experience for me to try to make people feel at ease while a camera was pointed at their faces. But it was interesting to start to understand how this different medium worked and the emotional power that could be captured in video files. The human voice and face convey a lot, not so much in terms of technical details, of course, but about our common humanity.

The challenges involved in the PR job increased rapidly not long after I took it up. The Great Recession had hit, and that meant the state's support of the university started to drop. Budget cuts were the order of the day, a challenging topic for any public relations agent to spin. There was still plenty of good work being done at the university by lots of people, of course, and the fund-raising mission was even more vital to the organization because of the increasing paucity of public funds.

One element of the PR job went well directly because of my old job at the local newspaper. After leaving the paper and coming back to the university I had continued to write my "Rock Doc" columns. I also expanded their focus from the area's local geology, things like garnet hunting to broader themes such as how Americans meet our national energy needs. While working in the PR business, I dreamed up the idea of offering the columns to other newspapers. Because of the internet and email, I realized, it would cost nothing to quickly distribute the columns to as many papers as might be interested in using them. My idea was not to charge the papers for the work, but just require them to run a tagline giving Washington State University credit for the pieces. Between that and the occasional column in which I interviewed a WSU scientist, the Rock Doc pieces would be a good – and essentially free – means of outreach in a manner not used by public relations personnel anywhere else that I knew about.

I explained my idea to my assistant and she undertook the task of gathering the names of editors and their addresses from papers all around the Pacific Northwest. We then wrote a letter to each editor, offering the column for distribution. Because the columns were free to the papers and likely because no other newspaper columnists dealt with topics relating to science, we started to hear back positively from community papers. Thus, within just a few weeks, the "Rock Doc" effort became a small but growing syndicated operation.

When I'd conceived of the idea of offering the columns to other papers, I'd decided I should write a column every week to help meet the needs of editors. Thus, I settled down to weekly production of the pieces while my assistant industriously launched herself into researching editors and papers in California and the Southwest. We wrote to those papers, just as we had earlier done to Northwest publications. Soon "Rock Doc Nation" was growing substantially and we could claim dozens of community newspapers with hundreds of thousands of total readers.

Next, my assistant went to work researching papers in the Great Plains. Then it was on to Texas and next to the Midwest. Finally, there was New England and all the states in the Southeast. Over several months, and owing to the diligence of my assistant who did the lion's share of the work, we contacted hundreds of newspapers. In the end over 200 papers had access to the weekly columns, papers with a combined circulation of over 2 million. In short, the newspaper outreach involved a lot of work – the production of the weekly column was not always child's play – but it was a way of getting visibility for my university for readers all across the country, and it did so with no distribution cost. Naturally, we set up a website highlighting the work, and my assistant even Tweeted the column's subject each time we released one. I felt a lot of satisfaction about the work we did producing and promoting the "Rock Doc" pieces, and my supervisor, the Dean of Science, seemed delighted with our success.

One day while walking with my dog I came up with a new idea for the Rock Doc pieces. I thought I should read them aloud and record the essays. My idea was that my assistant and I could feature the recordings on the website and, with luck, perhaps I could convince the local public radio station to broadcast at least some of them. I began to record the columns and found that, to my surprise, I was really nervous in front of a microphone.

The first recordings I made were a little short of awful, full of the tension I felt when trying to sound natural. But I persevered and gradually improved. Still, I didn't think the recordings were good enough to put on the website. My assistant politely agreed. For a time, the effort stalled. But later, when I suggested the idea of recording the columns to the director of the public radio station housed at the university, he thought it was a notion worth pursuing.

A woman named Robin Rylette, who was the announcer for the station's classical music programs, agreed to be my guide to the world of radio. Meeting with Robin, I was initially as nervous as I had been when trying to make recordings by myself. But she quickly put me at ease with stories about what it had been like for her to sit in front of a microphone when she began her career. Soon enough we had made several recordings. With Robin editing out the places where I had flubbed a word, the audio files didn't sound so bad. The following

Saturday morning Northwest Public Radio broadcast the first of our files and my presence in radio was begun.

At home I continued to work on my book. The climate change manuscript was taking full shape – or at least I thought so at the time. The agent in New York who had represented my murder mystery efforts had died several years previously, so I didn't have him to discuss the project I'd been working on diligently in the early mornings. I contacted my earlier agency, but the person who had inherited my account didn't think another offering on climate was likely what the book market needed. That meant I should either throw out the manuscript or find a new agent.

I began a small campaign of writing to agents in New York, introducing myself, sketching the manuscript I had written, and asking about potential interest in representing the book. Most of the agents to whom I wrote did not respond at all. A few gave me polite refusals, citing the mountain of books that had already been published on some aspect of climate. One of the very few who seriously tried to understand what I had written was a man named Russell Galen. Soon Russ and I were engaged in a series of long emails to one another.

From the start, Russ made it clear he thought the basic premise of the manuscript was incoherent. My book covered climate change and delved into national energy policies. Russ thought the book should be about climate, period. He also recommended I rewrite it so it was less like a lecture on what I thought people should understand about climate and, instead, told the story of how geologists and other scientists had learned about climate change. What was the evidence that had swayed early researchers, and how had their thinking developed? In short, Russ wanted the book to be a narrative of what had been discovered, rather than a more academic lecture organized by topics and subtopics. He said the way it was written it could find a publisher, but it wouldn't sell more than a few thousand copies. If I wanted to potentially take my writing to the next level, he argued, I should rewrite the book as a narrative of how geologists had learned what we know about both rapid and more gradual climate change.

I thought Russ made a good point. I also knew it would be a great deal of work to follow his advice. In general, scientists are not taught the history of how our fields develop. We are taught scientific content, but not the story of how generations of scientists have advanced knowledge. To do as he asked, I would have to research the history of how geologists had unearthed major findings about climate change. Then I'd have to turn that material into a story interesting enough that lay readers would be willing to follow me through the history of geologic discovery from the 1830s to the 21st century. But although the advice would not be easy to follow, I also suspected it was sound. People do like stories. And, to put the matter bluntly, Russell Galen was the only agent seriously advising me about how to proceed with my writing. I valued the time he had invested in our emails, and I wanted that relationship to continue.

Soon I was fully launched into the massive rewrite project. I spent Saturdays in the university's science library, ultimately checking out dozens of volumes and borrowing others through interlibrary loans. I was always on the lookout for a good tidbit regarding how research had been done or what the geologists who performed the work had really been like. I read biographies of geologists and talked time and time again with the faculty member at the university who taught the history of science. One good sign about the work, I thought, was that once I got started, I found it quite interesting. In some ways, how geologists learned about climate change was at least as gripping to me as what they had discovered about the planet's variability. And, using the years of practice I had accrued while teaching freshman geology, I seemed able to explain the evidence geologists had discovered in a way I hoped an interested layman could fathom.

Writing a manuscript with the structure Russ had suggested was my moonlighting job. My day job was still the PR gig. I was busy at work, but usually only during the normal 40-hour workweek. I was caring for my mother who lived in my house, but she was still well enough that she took herself to the doctors and kept track of her own medication. It was a good period, with mental illness always in the background but not exploding into my life. There were, however, times with rattlesnakes on the floor during the day, and on the floor around my bed at night. And now and then ordinary sounds blossomed into intense messages meant for me, although encoded in a language I could not understand. I did my best to cope with these fragments of psychosis, but the auditory hallucinations were hard to bear. As always, my mother's emotional support was helpful to me, and she was close at hand each day because she lived in my home. So, through this period I may not have been well, but I remained functional. But a new round of mental illness soon overtook me, leading to a substantial change in my diagnosis.

CHAPTER 6:

A NEW DIAGNOSIS

It was the winter of 2009 when I first knew something was amiss. My physical energy levels started to climb. At the gym I found I could lift more weight than normal. Instead of struggling to do my allotted number of curl-ups, I could easily add to the total of what I expected of myself, doing a couple hundred curl-ups with ease. Like many people who exercise seriously in middle age, I was surprised to find I was growing stronger rapidly. From age 40 onward it had been such a struggle to simply maintain my strength, I was glad to find I could – for some reason – actually add to it substantially. Still, I also worried about why I was getting so much stronger. While my mood was good, images of what was likely to come started to shift around uneasily at the edges of my mind.

But that January was a time in our life as a nation that seemed to me quite good. I've always been a politically aware and active citizen, with lifelong commitments to the spectrum's progressive end and religious concerns to match. Because of my political beliefs, George W. Bush's presidency had been a deeply distressing time for me, and our invasion of Iraq was the lowest point of my life as an American. In response to it, as a matter of religious conscience, I had chosen to object to the war in a manner that pacifists sometimes do.

After the Iraq war had begun, and continuing through all the time that President Bush was in office, I was what some Quakers and other low-church Christians call a "war tax resister." As such, I filed my federal income tax forms each year, but I adjusted my withholding status with my employer so that the money I owed to the federal government was still in my hands on April 15. When I filed my 1040 form, I included a letter saying I would not pay what I owed because of my deep objections to the war. Equally important to me, I sent a copy of the letter to each of my Congressional representatives and to the President.

While these actions may seem extreme, all I can say is that I tried to follow my conscience. Whether a natural gift for risk-taking was also at play in my protest is a question that comes to mind. For what it's worth, I had discussed the matter with my psychiatrist, who thought my actions were informed by values rather than illness.

The IRS does not view tax protestors kindly, no matter their motivation. While I was a war tax resister, I lived with the consequences of my actions. The Revenue Service assigned me penalties and interest, then put liens on my checking and saving accounts, reducing my balances to zero. In response, I closed the accounts and started living in a 100% cash economy. The IRS next put a lien on an IRA account of mine. When it was depleted, the Revenue Service started to garnish my salary. Throughout this time, in addition to the obvious expense and inconvenience of my status, I also lived with the fact that the government could choose at any time to pursue criminal prosecution in my case.

So, I had more than one reason to be glad when President Bush's term in office came to an end. For me, the first inauguration of Barack Obama was welcome both for abstract ideological reasons and because I knew I would be able to start cooperating once more with federal taxes, restoring my personal and financial life to a more secure foundation. And as frosting on the cake, I had strongly supported Obama throughout the primaries and the general election. On election day, I was a volunteer poll watcher in Idaho on behalf of the Democratic party. So, around the time of the presidential inaugural in January of 2009, I had good reasons to be on a steady emotional high. My uplifted feelings were particularly notable when I was working out at the gym. The blend of surging physical and emotional energy was agreeable, and when I wasn't worried about what I was experiencing, I could simply enjoy the feeling that life was deeply good.

But as the winter of the Obama inauguration continued, my physical energy increased still more. In short order, it moved from being a pleasure to being bothersome. As the energy mounted yet higher, it became fully problematic. At the gym, I was drenched in sweat. In my office, it was difficult to sit still. My old nemesis, insomnia, engulfed me. Without a decent night's sleep, I was soon feeling a deep sense of alarm. At unpredictable times my adrenalin levels soared, and mental rattlesnakes swarmed over the floor around me. For the first time in my life, I clearly and consciously wondered if my high-energy suffering could be a form of mania, rather than the depression doctors had always told me I suffered from. I don't know where that idea came from, and I didn't know how to evaluate the notion. But the concept of mania floated around in my mind, another element of my distress because I knew so little about what it might mean.

The winter evolved into a spring crisis. One day at work I spoke on the phone about my increasing torment with a friend from church. She listened to what I was reporting about my rapidly escalating distress, and perhaps she listened more to my exhausted and desperate tone. Luckily, she had the courage to act on what she heard and called my psychiatrist's office. As it happened, the doctor had a cancellation that very afternoon and my friend called me back with the news. Mumbling hasty apologies to my assistant, I left work for the one-hour drive south to the small city where my doctor practiced.

Psychiatrists are particularly alert to what may happen when a patient appears in their schedule outside an appointment scheduled long in advance. As I explained my energy levels and insomnia to the doctor, he listened intently and patiently. I asked him if I were manic. He said no, he didn't think so, but he also made time in his schedule for me to come back two days later and see him again. I was glad to think I wasn't suffering from mania, a state I knew little about but feared. I was also grateful for the quick follow-up appointment because it gave me something to hold onto in the teeth of the storm.

When I returned to the doctor's office two days later, I found his thinking and his manner were noticeably different. He no longer spoke quietly nor gently to me. He had dug out the record of my hospitalization in 1997 in the locked ward associated with his clinic, and he read to me a quotation of what I had said in the emergency room. At that time, in my distress, I had said I "felt like I was going to explode."

Rather triumphantly, the psychiatrist explained that my crisis at that time was now happening to me once again. My problem, he said, was not depression, as all the previous doctors going back to my days as a student had always maintained. Feeling that an internal explosion was imminent is a high-energy, not a low-energy, state. Fixing me with glittering eyes across the small consulting room, the psychiatrist told me I had bipolar disorder.

I knew next to nothing about bipolar disorder as a diagnosis, but I wanted to reject the idea of being manic-depressive if I could.

"No, no, no," I said with only emotional conviction on my side, "I don't want to be bipolar."

"Then we'll just call it something else," he shot back tersely.

The doctor's brusque retort took me up short, and I became quiet. He told me that because I had bipolar disorder, I needed to start different types of medications from any I had ever tried. I would have to give up my favorite anti-depressant, Remeron, which had made the transition from part-time to full-time work possible when I was in my late 30s. Remeron was the drug that from my perspective gave me more mental clarity than any other I knew, the one that had all but eliminated suicidal thoughts from my life. I was staggered to even consider losing that medication, but the doctor was insistent. The reason for the radical change in my pharmaceutical life, he explained, was that anti-depressants are known to make bipolar people manic. The problem I was having as we sat there together, he explained, was fueled by manic energy.

In the months after that day, I researched bipolar illness, reading books and technical articles about it like any good scientist should. I came to realize the diagnosis made more sense than anything people in the mental health industry had said to me in the previous 30 years, even though it also did not have much room within it for my hearing things or living with rattlesnakes on the floor. But the diagnosis gave me a framework to explain at least a couple of parts of my internal life. And I came to realize that manic states don't have to be joyful, but rather they can be high-energy misery, what's known as dysphoric mania. That explained so well how I can always fight with sleeplessness and walking all over creation while feeling terrible in emotional terms.

Both laymen and medical authorities can agree, bipolar disease runs in families. As I researched the condition, I learned that the reason manic depressives cluster in families is due to genes, not childhood experiences. After accepting the diagnosis and learning about the strong genetic link to the illness, I was relieved. It meant I no longer had to spend time and energy thinking my illness was the result of weak will or bad habits. It wasn't that I had had a poor upbringing, nor could I become well just by reading the right self-help book or eating more vegetables. I was ill for the same reason I had brown hair and hazel eyes – it was just how I was put together. Nature, not nurture, not personal failings, not bad habits of thought, had made me ill.

As I sat in the narrow consultation room with the psychiatrist the day, he announced I was a person with bipolar disorder, my understanding of manic-depressive illness was negligible. When the doctor testily told me the nature of my illness, I was thoroughly disoriented, as well as simply afraid. I suspect now the doctor was brusque with me because he knew he was rendering a verdict on my life that brought with it what can only be called a challenging prognosis. Many people with bipolar disorder suffer more and more deeply from the disease as they age. The death rate from the malady is impressive, and lifespan is seriously shortened.

While psychiatrists never have to tell people they have a malignancy, pronouncing the diagnosis of bipolar illness may pain them in the same way oncologists suffer when they deliver bad news. Of course, that's not to say being ill-tempered when giving a patient such a diagnosis is professionally defensible. But at a human level, I can at least understand part of what likely ailed my psychiatrist the significant day we sat across from each other and he told me what he thought my illness was. Years later I got a copy of my medical records from the clinic where the psychiatrist practiced. I was interested to see his notes from our meetings which spanned several years. It was clear in the written record that from our very first meeting, he was considering the bipolar diagnosis. My earlier, repeated hospitalizations were one clue, although recurrent depression could also lead to a long hospitalization record. But as the doctor knew me better and watched me climb into a high-energy state in the spring of 2009, he decided I was bipolar, not depressed.

In many ways, the new diagnosis vindicated my suspicions that I was quite different from most people around me. The "normal people," as I had always called others, didn't experience episodes of searing sunlight in their skulls or hear maniacal laughter ringing in their ears. At one level it was a relief to know I wasn't like the normal people – and I didn't therefore have to pretend I was one of them any longer. In that respect, the diagnosis took considerable weight off my shoulders.

After telling me his new diagnosis, the psychiatrist insisted I start taking an anti-seizure drug given to patients with bipolar disorder. It wasn't that I'd ever had any problems with seizures, it's simply that doctors give bipolar patients medications from the anti-seizure group of drugs because they can help moderate mental states. There are several anti-seizure medications on the market. The one my psychiatrist picked for me was a common one called Depakote, a medication you could say is like the aspirin of the anti-seizure group, it's so common and well-known in the psychiatric community.

But the fact that a bipolar drug is common doesn't mean it's easy to survive. Depakote proved to be the toughest medication I had taken up to that point.

For several days I literally staggered under its influence because it made me unsteady on my feet. Worse, for close to three months, I was profoundly nauseated each day in the early afternoon. I adjusted my work schedule and moved to what was essentially a split shift, going home from work at midday not for lunch, which I was too ill to eat, but so I could lie on the sofa as nausea washed over me. When I could get up again, I would go back to work, glad I lived in a small town in which making the roundtrip commute twice a day was no problem. The drug also gave me a new sensation in my skull. The only way to describe it is to say the top of my brain felt like it had been wrinkled but was now becoming smooth. The psychiatrist wasn't surprised by anything I reported in terms of side effects, and he seemed positively pleased about the smooth sensation of my brain.

Soon I found that Depakote also had strong, if transitory, mental effects. After a couple of weeks on the drug, I started to experience two hours of euphoria each day. To be sure, I was still suffering extremely for 22 hours out of each 24. But I came to count on those two hours of deep joy each day, and I'm sure the hours of morning euphoria helped me to cope with my new diagnosis. I didn't mention the joy to the psychiatrist because I'm no fool even when I'm remarkably ill. I didn't want him to adjust the dose of the drug or substitute something else for Depakote, not if it meant losing those positive feelings. I figured I needed those two hours to see me through if I had to suffer so much for most of the day – and all of the night. And, as I've discovered, many a psych patient doesn't mention euphoria to doctors, particularly if it doesn't affect how one functions in the world.

One day Depakote changed my visual perception in a way that was unlike anything I'd known in the past. On Easter Sunday that spring, I visited good friends in the country, walking with them around their house, up a small valley, and then back to where they lived. They have always fed a variety of birds, and perhaps because of their rural location, they have quite an avian clientele.

I did a double-take when I looked at a goldfinch and saw it was an indescribably intense yellow, brighter than the yellow sun, incomparable to any other color I'd ever seen before. Repeated observations as we walked showed that all the songbirds that Sunday afternoon were colored in delightfully powerful hues. That experience only lasted a day, so I didn't need to hide it from the psychiatrist lest he take it away from me. I therefore described it to him when next we met. He saw it as the effect of a manic state, and while I granted that could well be the case, I also noted it was an experience I'd never had before taking Depakote, indicating to me that the drug – not just illness alone – was in some sense triggering it.

When Depakote was first prescribed to me, both the psychiatrist and the psychologist said that my adjustment period would be about three months. But as I neared the three-month mark, I noted they switched to saying that it would take three to six months for me to get used to it. And then, around half a year after I had begun, they simply said that it took a year to adjust to an anti-seizure drug like Depakote. While I didn't appreciate their misleading me – and I still don't – I have to admit my journey from the seventh to the eighth month of the drug was vastly easier than from the first to the second. I also admit that I never would have persevered if I had known I was facing a rough trip for a full year. I may be a fairly stubborn individual, used to setting goals and attaining them, but I'm sure I just would not have made it for so long given how ill Depakote made me.

Depakote hardly cured my troubles, but it did have some positive effects. My diagnosis occurred in the spring. By the end of the summer, I realized I was sleeping many hours each night, and slumbering deeply. Instead of dreading nights spent tossing and turning, as I had done for literally decades, I simply went to bed and fell asleep. The transition was astounding for an insomniac with 30 years of sleeplessness under her belt.

High doses of Depakote had another clear benefit. The normal people around me have always appeared to slow down from time to time, speaking and making decisions at a snail's pace. On Depakote, I could wait for the normal people to slog through the molasses that occasionally engulfs them, without feeling the burning impatience I had known for so many years. That change, in turn, meant I didn't have to invest my emotional energy in remaining polite around incredibly slow people. Simply put, I was at peace with the intervals of retardation from which the normal people sometimes suffered. Like sleeping at night, the change was blissful.

But I was far from well. Under the influence of high-doses of Depakote,

I stumbled and fell to the floor several times. Around my house, I was prevented from falling only by holding out a hand to steady myself against a nearby wall. Then one day I fell badly on the railroad tracks down by the Snake River where I go to walk my dog on the weekends. I broke my fall with my right hand, jamming a knuckle joint and badly bruising my palm in the process. Nothing was broken, but my finger joint ached for months.

But I had to adjust to more than side effects. After following the psychiatrist's directions and tapering off the anti-depressant medications I had been on for years, I started feeling melancholy. The treatment for that, the psychiatrist said, was to add to my new regimen a drug from yet another class, namely the atypical antipsychotics.

The drugs get their imposing name simply because they have replaced problematic antipsychotics that came earlier. The first family of antipsychotics that came earlier in the history of medicine developed around the middle of the twentieth century, are now known as "typical" ones, and the newer medications, which have come out nearer to the turn of the century, are called "atypical" antipsychotics. Like the anti-seizure drugs, the atypical are given to people who may not be psychotic. Prescriptions are written at times simply in an attempt to rearrange brain chemistry in one direction or another. My doctor gave me atypical antipsychotics in an attempt to lessen the depression I was experiencing.

The first medication we tried kept me in bed for several days, so strong was its sedating effect. We therefore gave up that experiment and moved on to a second drug. Taking that particular antipsychotic was a process that stretched from weeks to months, resulting in both a strong tremor and a head of curly hair. While I loved the latter effect, the former was more than annoying, and I soon was calling the atypical antipsychotics "the evil drugs."

The drug trials were not easy. But at work things were going well. One day in the spring of 2010, I received a phone call from a fellow public relations professional at WSU. She was and is an able and accomplished woman, tall and well-dressed. She was at that time the director of public relations for the College of Agriculture, the largest division within the university. She had a question for me: would I possibly be interested in changing jobs and becoming a grant writer?

She said the associate dean for research in her college was looking to set up a new office to support faculty members as they submitted enormous and complex grant proposals that were becoming the norm. While in the old days, grants from the federal government often involved just one faculty researcher and ran to the hundreds of thousands of dollars, the research game was changing – and rapidly so. The Department of Agriculture and the Department of Energy, among other granting agencies in D.C., were increasingly looking to fund projects undertaken by large consortia of faculty researchers with budgets that ran into the tens of millions of dollars. They did so because of their belief that solving societal problems – like producing cheaper green energy from biofuels – could best be done by large, transdisciplinary groups of researchers.

I certainly had never considered being a grant writer, but I also was glad to think of new possibilities in my working life. I told my colleague I would indeed be interested in exploring a novel avenue of work. She said she would pass along that reply. In time I got a call from the Associate Dean for Agriculture. Ralph Cavalieri said he was looking for a science writer for the grant writer position, and he wondered if we could talk. He volunteered that he could come to my office. There was no reason to do that, I quickly said, I would be pleased to walk over to his.

When I met with Ralph it became clear he wanted to hire someone who could start to work for him right away. In just a few months a $45 million grant proposal was scheduled to be submitted to the government, and the work involved in putting together that package was going to be a significant undertaking by any measure. We talked about my background in grants. I had helped to turn in a grant proposal at Harvard, and I'd turned in two of my own later in life as an instructor. But as I freely admitted to Ralph, nothing I had known even approached involvement in a complex proposal with dozens of researchers. That, however, wasn't a problem from his point of view. The mega-proposals were brand new to his faculty, and he didn't expect me to be an expert in their preparation before I had even begun. The person Ralph thought he was looking for would be an editor and a flexible generalist, someone who could help put together the proposals from soup-to-nuts.

When it became clear that Ralph wanted to hire me, I mentioned I had an assistant I would want to bring with me into any new job. And Susan, as it happened, had considerable experience in supporting faculty proposals to the National Institute of Health and the National Science Foundation. Ralph liked the sound of that and said if I would accept the job working for him, I could bring Susan along for the ride.

In short order I found myself saying goodbye to my colleagues in the College of Science and plunging into the new job. It was an exciting, but also stressful time. I was a babe in the woods, working with faculty who had never done proposals on the scale we were now supposed to wrestle with. There were more questions than answers and, indeed, there were days when neither the faculty nor I knew exactly how to frame the questions which we should be addressing.

Unfortunately, in my initial weeks in the new job, when I felt plenty of stress, I also had to change the psychiatric drugs I was taking. I had been suffering from an increasingly problematic tremor that seemed to be linked to my medications. My psychiatrist instructed me to gradually cut down on my anti-seizure drug, which he suspected of causing the tremor. And as I tapered down on that drug, the doctor gave me a new anti-seizure medication to start slowly. This maneuver, known as a "double taper," is never easy. The side effects of the new medication are likely to be felt before any potential good effects are, and if the drug being phased out had actually been doing some good, those effects may well be lost before the new drug has enough time to take hold.

Throughout June I went through the double taper. Unfortunately, at the end of the maneuver, I still had the tremor that led the doctor to say I should stop the original anti-seizure drug. Therefore, the grief I'd been through substituting the anti-seizure medications had been for naught. The psychiatrist said I should stay on the new anti-seizure drug because I was established on it. My tremor, he then announced, was either caused by the atypical antipsychotic medication I was taking or, perhaps, I was starting to experience Parkinson's. To check out the latter possibility I should see a neurologist.

There was no denying I had an intrusive tremor. My stress level went through the roof at the mention it might be caused by Parkinson's. Luckily, the neurologist I called had a chance of opening in just a few days. I soon was in his waiting room, wondering if my medical life was about to become vastly more complicated. But the tremor, the neurologist said, might well be caused by the atypical antipsychotic medication I was still taking. He had seen tremors just like mine linked to drugs in that class. He urged me to taper down and off the drug in question. I reported the neurologist's findings and recommended a course of action to the psychiatrist, who agreed with them. A few weeks after I was off the atypical antipsychotic, my tremor gradually subsided. Eventually, it disappeared almost entirely.

My medication regimen had been changed twice in two months. Following the instructions of the two doctors, I had swapped one anti-seizure medication for another, and I had stopped taking the antipsychotic agent I'd been on for most of a year. By mid-August the tremor was subsiding and I thought I was out of the woods. Nothing could have been further from the truth.

On a Friday afternoon at work, I was sitting in a meeting concerning a multimillion-dollar grant proposal when the speed of my thinking violently exploded. One thought led to another more quickly than I could follow. Luckily, the meeting was coming to an end and it was near the end of the work day. I made my excuses and left my office, hoping to get home before anything worse knocked me off my feet. I was in tears when I walked through my front door. My thinking was no longer crazily rapid, but it was intense enough I couldn't eat my supper that evening. I took tranquilizers and got some sleep. In the morning, things in my head were a bit better, and I was able to work all weekend on the large grant proposal then on my desk. I accomplished a lot over the weekend and by Sunday night I thought the matter was behind me.

But the following days and weeks continued problematic. My physical energy started to mount. I met the major deadline at work we'd been working toward all summer, and I felt good about that. But when I took a few days off to relax, I wasn't able to slow down. Soon the energy in me was growing to absurd proportions. By October, I could swim and walk for hours and not be tired. I started to lose weight despite eating four meals a day. Time and time again, I reported my problems to the psychiatrist's office by telephone, but the instructions always came back to simply take more of the anti-seizure medication I was on. Alas, taking larger and larger doses of it did no good.

When I started to sleep less and less, I quickly spiraled upward into a dysphoric manic state. I was exhausted and desperate, no medication I had on hand would slow me down, not even my strongest tranquilizer. Talking the matter over with the local psychologist, we decided there was no help for it but to go to the hospital and become an in-patient in the psych ward where I had been hospitalized 13 years previously. Once I was in the hospital, we both knew, my medications could be changed – and the changes would be made at a much more rapid clip than anything the psychiatrist would attempt if I remained an outpatient. So, it was that I called my friend and former colleague at the newspaper, Steve, and asked for a ride to the hospital. He answered his phone immediately and said he'd be right over to pick me up.

At first, my main goal after gingerly getting into Steve's low-slung car was simply to refrain from throwing up. Steve cheerfully said that he, too, hoped I might show restraint in that department. Things went remarkably well once we were underway through the countryside of southeast Washington.

Having made the difficult decision to go to the hospital and having successfully found a ride to get there, I became calmer and more centered. Soon Steve's old car was sweeping down more than 1,500 feet in elevation, coasting at 60 mph from the plateau where we live to

Lewiston, a small city at the confluence of two major rivers, the Snake and the Clearwater. We quickly reached the hospital. After I checked in at the front desk, I turned and gave Steve a hug. But even as I embraced him, I felt distinctly and painfully separated from him. There is a gulf that lies between people with a major mental illness and those who never experience abnormal psychiatric states. Still, I know it's really not Steve's fault he's what I call a "normal person," one who doesn't take spontaneous and life-threatening trips of the mind.

Steve lives, like so many of my friends, on the right side of the psychiatric tracks. I admit I often envy the normal people who spend their lives seriously removed from me and my kind. They don't have to cope with the sometimes terror and maddening pain that marks the existence of those in the grips of major mental illness. Normal people aren't labeled with an imaginary yet clear tag on their foreheads, a label associated with shooting sprees in schools and shopping malls. Another difference between us is that folks on the right side of the tracks can reasonably predict what their lives will be like next month. My fellow patients and I must qualify all our hopes and plans by acknowledging that no matter how well we are doing at the moment, and no matter what treatment plan we follow, we could be dramatically ill once more at any time. Even when we emerge from downturns with our jobs and homes intact, my counterparts and I must cope with shaken self-confidence and staggering medical bills.

In some moods, I've been known to resent the normal people. There are so many of them, that I feel I'm immersed in a sea of Others as large as the Pacific. The normal people don't pace all night, but often go to bed and actually sleep straight through until the morning, a feat I've only accomplished occasionally, usually when I've been seriously drugged. The speed and nature of normal people's thoughts, apparently, are rather constant, not exploding into warp drive without warning or careening off into detailed plans for self-destruction despite every conscious effort to avoid such thinking. Their thoughts don't plummet on a pleasant Saturday morning down into a canyon of self-torture for no reason they can discern. The normal people don't have day-dreams of suicide gnawing at their consciousness as they try to concentrate enough to work, nor do they look at the psychotic homeless on a city sidewalk and instantly understand such a life could be theirs.

But although envy and resentment mark some of my thoughts about normal people, I often enough am glad to be indebted to them. From long experience, I know I need the folks on the right side of the tracks. Every time I lurch into a crisis, I reach out to them for help, and I truly need it as I attempt to survive the fresh ordeal into which my unstable brain chemistry has dropped me. Getting to the hospital that autumn day before I committed suicide made me deeply grateful to Steve, and I tried to tell him that as we parted. He didn't fully understand what was at issue – the normal people really never do – but my debt was clear to me, and it made me grateful not just to Steve, but to all of his kind.

Then it was time to push the buzzer and walk through the locked steel door that separates people like me inside the award from the world of the normal people outside the institution. The transition through the divide the heavy door represents is painful and abrupt, but in some ways, it is also welcome. I know and love plenty of normal people. Some of my best friends are normal people. But it's also true that I understand folks with major mental illness a good bit better. And beyond simple understanding, I have a special respect for many of the patients I've met in locked psychiatric wards. The courage that mental patients – especially those who have lived their whole lives in poverty – display is as heartening as anything I've ever seen in this complex world. But even so, hearing the heavy metal door of a psych ward click shut behind you isn't a welcoming sound. Walking into a locked unit is emotionally intense, a deeply difficult experience even for those of us who have made the journey several times.

Step One in a psychiatric ward means submitting to a search. Staffers take away your cell phone, any pocket knives or street drugs you have on you, and all prescription medications you may have brought with you to the ward. They also take away things with which you could try to hang yourself: belts, drawstrings on pants or pajamas, and shoelaces. Moving around in shoes without laces can be a tripping hazard, so some patients opt to walk around just in socks or slippers, if they thought to bring the latter with them to the hospital.

Shortly after the nurse searched me, and despite tears of exhaustion, I asked for pen and paper. Sitting down at the simple desk in my narrow hospital room with paper and a cheap ballpoint pen, I began to write a letter that I hoped would get to Princeton. The letter was to my undergraduate advisor's wife.

Sarah has been significant to me for decades. With her training as a psychiatric social worker and experience working in a mental hospital, in recent years she has been a cross between a friend and a personal advisor for my life as a mental patient. One of the few benefits of having my illness is the energy it often pours into me, and I was fueled by manic intensity as I started to scribble words onto paper for Sarah. I most urgently wanted to convey to her that night that I had been faithfully taking my medication. On the telephone, she sometimes reminds me of the importance of taking the drugs prescribed by the psychiatrists. Those drugs have multiple side effects, and some of them cost the earth.

Many patients with major mental illnesses quit taking their medications because of the physical problems serious psychiatric drugs cause, because of their expense, or simply because taking pills every few hours grows tiresome. From the authorities' point of view in the mental health industry, "non-compliant" patients are both common and frustrating. Doctors and other professionals in the field like to believe their patients would be well, or at least well enough if only they would do what they are told. I was living proof that night that such is not always the case.

Although the drugs my psychiatrist had prescribed during the late summer of 2010 hadn't done me much if any good – as witnessed by the fact I had lost 10 pounds in a couple of weeks and was freshly arrived in the locked psychiatric ward – compliant I had surely been. That evening I strongly wanted credit in Sarah's book for doing what I had been told, even as I also wanted to explain to her just how fast I was falling into a new phase of illness, one with more strongly manic elements than I'd known in the past.

Writing is always useful to me, even when I'm announcing a personal disaster. There's something about translating experiences into words that can be laid out on a piece of paper that helps my peculiar brain. I explained to Sarah the depth of the abyss into which I was falling, and how I had sought refuge from my mind in a locked ward in Idaho. Although the letter detailed me at my worst, I felt calmer when I finished it, and I was able to stop crying. Getting up from the simple desk in my room, I walked the few steps required to get to the nurses' station at the front of the ward. There I bummed an envelope from a staffer.

Addressing the envelope to Sarah was a bit of a challenge. True, I've stayed in my advisor's home several times over the years, and I can picture it easily in my mind's eye. I could walk to it in the dark from Princeton University's campus, it's that clear in my memory. But I don't have the relevant house number memorized, and I certainly hadn't brought any personal records like an address book with me. So, I wrote out the envelope to Sarah in the care of her husband at Princeton University's geology department. Despite exhaustion and suffering, I can always write out a departmental address of my alma mater. Not for the first time I thought how fortunate I am to know people on the right side of the tracks, namely in the land of stable minds and permanent addresses. I had no stamps with me, but a kind nurse took the letter and said she'd put it in the ward's outgoing mail bin, automatically getting postage in the hospital's system of metering. It was late and I didn't have much hope of sleep, so I returned to my little room.

On the right as I entered the space was a small bathroom with stool, sink and shower. The shower curtain was held in place only by Velcro – there was no curtain rod because of the risk a patient like me would find a way to hang herself from it. Beyond the bathroom, on the left side of the room, was the desk I had used to write my letter. A couple of drawers below the writing surface served as a place to store clothes. Across from the desk was a twin bed, the head of which was beside a window. Because the psychiatric ward was on the hospital's fifth floor, the window – which could not be opened – looked out over the tops of lower buildings in the neighborhood, most of which were residential houses.

Although the psych ward was decidedly utilitarian in almost all respects, one element of luxury had been explained to me when I checked in. Each room belonging to a patient had an independent thermostat. I am a miserably cold sleeper, and it was well into the autumn, so I had elected to set the temperature in my room at a cozy 72 degrees. I turned off the overhead light but left on a special light built into the wall near knee level next to the door. With that as a nightlight I hoped would ward off some of my anxiety, I lay down on my hospital bed's amazingly thin and lumpy mattress. Because I was a veteran of stays in the psych ward, I had left my door to the hallway ajar. I knew the staff would be coming and going all night at regular intervals, checking on me with a flashlight as they did all the other patients, looking for signs of trouble, particularly preparations for suicide.

Sometimes, in my night terrors, I can't face trying to even lie down at bedtime. When I was younger, I would walk for miles through the early morning darkness outside. But in the hospital that particular night, I was able to take off my shoes and crawl into bed. I may have been fully clothed but, under the circumstances, lying down was a victory in itself. And perhaps because I was comforted by the notion that I'd told a lifelong friend where I was and what was once again happening to me, I actually did sleep for a couple of hours. Sometimes, even for people in a manic state, exhaustion is rewarded by the reprieve of temporary rest.

Life in a hospital pulls patients into the rhythms of the institution. Hours start to flow naturally into days for mental patients, just as for people who are recovering from surgery or childbirth. Meals help the institutionalized define and measure time. For mental patients, there is also the ticking metronome of daily group meetings. After various meetings and many meals, a fellow patient came to my little room to call me to the common telephone that hung in the hallway near the nurses' station.

My letter had reached Sarah, and she was calling from Princeton. In the odd world in which I live, it doesn't surprise me that the bonds I forged at college have spanned decades and possess the power to reach through the locked steel door of a psychiatric ward. In that respect, I take my personal good fortune in stride. I'm used to the fact that I made connections at both Princeton and Harvard and in my small hometown I have endured through times that even a crazy person considers rather extreme. But although I'm not surprised by events like cross-country telephone calls from the spouse of an advisor, I am deeply and profoundly grateful for them. I think the landscape of mental illness only becomes truly and finally hellish when connections with other people are lost.

As stays in locked psychiatric wards go, that one was reasonably pleasant. I was more manic than depressed. I didn't hear things. Lastly, I had good comrades around me. The staff had their quirks, but nothing major was amiss. My main accomplishment during my time in the hospital was quitting the anti-seizure drug I'd been on since mid-summer and ramping up the dosage of a new one. After about a week I was discharged to return to my home. I was glad to sleep in a better bed once more, and glad to see my friends, my family, and my dog. I returned to work and was welcomed back.

But within just a couple of days, I knew I was in for more problems. My emotional life was churning like a boiling cauldron. Soon I realized I was turning from a manic state to a depressive one. Luckily, I had a follow-up appointment with the psychiatrist not long after getting out of the hospital.

"Everything is changing," I said to him in his out-patient office, "and it's changing for the worse." I explained I had stopped exercising entirely – no swimming, no walking. In just two weeks, I'd gone from insane amounts of exercise to not having the energy to do anything. I tried to force myself to eat, but I wasn't able to get through a full meal. Finally, and most ominously, my thinking was deeply depressed and becoming more so each day.

"Just today it's occurred to me I may not live through this," I said.

The psychiatrist sat upright. "You mean by your own hand?" he asked.

"Yes," I said simply.

At my request, the psychiatrist wrote a prescription for the maximum dose of Remeron, the anti-depressant drug that had always helped me. He had taken me off Remeron 18 months earlier when he had diagnosed me with bipolar disorder. Doctors fear antidepressants can make people with bipolar disorder manic, so they often take patients off such drugs. But now our backs were against the wall with life-threatening depression washing over my head. So, armed with scripts for my favorite anti-depressant, I returned home.

Unfortunately, it takes time for anti-depressants to work, and I was getting rapidly worse. My thoughts were increasingly depressed and desperate. I called the psychiatrist's office and reported that each day was worse. The doctor prescribed Zoloft, a common anti-depressant, for me to add to my medication regime. I did so and was rewarded with headache and nausea, common responses to Zoloft. Over the weekend that followed, I started to see unbidden visions of death and think of specific ways I could kill myself. I felt like I was in free fall, and I knew it could be four to six weeks before the anti-depressants fully kicked in. I talked with my minister on Sunday afternoon. She gave me tea and advised me to go back to the hospital. But I stayed in my home that night, trying desperately to avoid institutionalization if I could.

As fate would have it, I was also coming down with a bad head cold that weekend. It didn't help my mood that I was coughing and blowing my nose. I took what cold medicine I had on hand in the bathroom cabinet, and tried to ignore my symptoms as best I could. But on Sunday night I slept very little, robbed of rest by the cold and my increasingly self-destructive thoughts.

On Monday, I was in a thick haze. I called in sick to work and collapsed on a futon in my home office. As I lay there, I was enveloped in a fog of depression, deeper than I'd known at any time since my Harvard days. More images of death came to me out of the fog. Dying looked like the one good option for escaping the suffering I was experiencing. I turned over in my mind how I could kill myself at home that very morning. I could douse myself with the gasoline that was in the garage and light a match. That would be a painful way of ending it all. To avoid such suffering, I could take all my pills – a considerable psych drug arsenal. Hazily I thought that I didn't necessarily want to die, I was simply indifferent to living. To die or not to die – I turned over the question in my foggy head. Time dragged on as I lay on the futon. I wondered when I would get up and what I might do when I did so.

Finally, I had the energy to sit up and take stock of what was happening. I realized I had the same choice I always had: I could choose the simplicity and finality of death or the narrow and rocky path of trying to live. Although I didn't feel terribly strongly about the matter, one way or another, I thought I wanted to choose life one more time if I could. I called the psychologist and explained the shape I was in. He called the psych ward and learned they had beds to spare. I made yet another phone call to get a ride to the hospital.

After that, there was nothing to do but explain to my mother that I was going back to the locked ward and get a few clothes together to take with me. Thus, it was that in just a couple of weeks, I went from being hospitalized in a manic state to crashing into a deeply depressed condition.

When I got back into the hospital the first question was which drugs should be continued and which should be dropped. Thankfully, the doctor who checked me in let me keep the two anti-depressants I had been taking at home. He stopped the anti-seizure drug I had been on, saying it clearly wasn't helping me. He left matters at that, so my own psychiatrist could make the all-important decisions about what new medications it made sense to try.

That first night in the hospital was a long one. I was blowing my nose every few minutes and trying to guard my thoughts against suicidal ideas. The poor mattress made rest seem impossible. I tossed and turned for hours, then finally got a nap. But just before dawn, things worsened considerably. I seemed to have a waking nightmare of a hurricane, an enormous storm pulverizing everything around me. The waves tossed broken boats; the water was filled with dead bodies.

The terror I felt was like that commonly experienced in nightmares, but I knew I was fully awake and lying in bed in the psych ward. Then a dark cloud swept over me, pinning me to my bed. It felt like the finality of death was holding me down. I couldn't move or call out, even though I knew a nurse must be nearby. There was nothing I could do, immobilized as I was, but to wait for the experience to pass. As the light of a November dawn finally filtered into the room, the waking nightmare faded into memory and the dark cloud in my mind dissipated. With relief, I found I could move my limbs again.

When my psychiatrist arrived in the morning to do his rounds, we met with each other in an interview room. I put a lot of my limited energy into trying to describe to him what the fog was like in which I'd been enveloped as I lay on the futon in my home and what the waking nightmare and dark cloud had been like in the hospital just before dawn. I had my head in my hands as I talked, trying my best to explain both what I'd been through and how close I was to the end of what I'd be able to bear.

The question of what drugs I should take turned out to be a bone of contention between the doctor and me. We could agree on dropping the anti-seizure drug that had done no good. But the psychiatrist wanted me to try another drug from the class that had given me the tremor from which I had only recently escaped: another atypical antipsychotic. From my point of view, I was ramping up two antidepressants as rapidly as possible, and I didn't want to add another drug to the mix – particularly one from a class that had given me debilitating physical side effects. I needed time for the antidepressants to work, and if I could avoid it, I didn't want to complicate that interval with a new drug. I have a copy of my doctor's notes from that hospitalization. They show he started discussing the matter of adding an atypical antipsychotic to my medications the first day we spoke to one another. That fits with my memory of what became a rift between us. I wanted time for the anti-depressants to work, while he wanted to throw a wholly new medication into the mix to see how I might respond. We met with each other each business day I was hospitalized and we argued out the question, again and again. I was adamant. I thought I might well die when I got out of the hospital. If I were to do so I wanted to perish of the disease I knew so well and with medications I also knew – not a new agent I thought likely to make me physically ill with major tremors and potentially distort my mind in ways I could not predict. In the end, I compromised. I said I'd try a new anti-seizure agent, but not another atypical antipsychotic. That didn't satisfy the doctor at all. But throughout that long and miserable hospitalization, I only took the medications I wanted. I was terribly ill, with waking nightmares and psychotic experiences in the exercise room where I thought there were wonderful angelic beings behind a sheetrock wall, but I didn't waver in what I wanted on the medication front. Even when gravely ill, I can be enormously stubborn.

Unfortunately, my psychiatrist let his feelings get in the way of any treatment he could offer me. He often spoke testily when we met for our one-on-one interviews each day. His anger hurt me keenly at the time. Earlier, I had looked up to him because he was the doctor who had given me the diagnosis of being bipolar, an insight that although not perfect had explained more than all earlier diagnoses that I was simply depressed.

The doctor's anger now cut me to the quick. Looking back at it from a safe distance, I can imagine that it was his concern for a patient he genuinely liked, one who had fallen into life-threatening depression, that caused him to be angry. His primary emotion, as the mental health gurus would say, was fear or helplessness. But anger was his secondary emotion, and that's the one he felt free to express to me, an expression that was clearly unprofessional. In short, he was not separating his feelings from my situation.

Anger was a close companion of the doctor, as shown by one snippet of a conversation we had about suicide while I was in the locked ward. He said, "If you kill yourself, I will be pissed off." I replied, "I hope you would be grieved, not 'pissed off'." He replied, "That, too." I truly suffered from the doctor's anger. I was in a deep depression and in a locked ward, making me completely vulnerable to how the authorities around me acted. One day in our one-on-one sessions, the doctor asked me what felt like an impossible question. He said, "Have I ever given you a reason to distrust me?" I felt that each instance of his anger meant that he had done exactly that. But as his patient in a locked ward, I couldn't say "Yes, you give exactly that." But as his patient in a locked ward, I couldn't say "Yes, you give me reason to distrust you most days we meet." So, I gave an evasive answer similar to what a politician might give at a press conference to a query he does not want to address. The doctor repeated his question. With quiet desperation, I repeated my evasion. He replied, "I'll take that as a 'no.'"

My analysis now of that exchange – initiated by the doctor – is that at some level he must have known he was out of line in the manner he had been speaking with me. His question to me, likely unprofessional in itself when asked of a patient in a deep depression in a locked ward, reflected his own criticism at some level of himself.

My problems with my doctor during that hospitalization added substantially to my suffering. Enduring the interviews with the doctor came to be a burden. But surviving sojourns in psych wards always takes a lot of endurance. For one thing, there are some basic physical issues in the ward. The hospital mattress I had to sleep on was both painfully thin and lumpy.

Worse, the nurses came into patients' rooms regularly throughout the night to check on the status of people who might be trying to figure out ways to harm themselves. There's nothing like having a flashlight on your face regularly to rob you of the rest you need. In short, it's almost inevitable a person becomes physically worn down by the conditions of a psych ward.

But there were some better times, too, in the hospital. Several revolved around visitors, some of whom came time and time again to see me while I was locked up. All visitors to locked wards are precious and valued. But in that long hospitalization, I was particularly impressed by the generosity of a colleague who came to see me one evening. At least for a professional person, there is something about a visit from someone you know from work that helps combat the erosion of self-worth it's easy enough to feel in a psych ward. I had contacted my colleague via a friend who called me on the telephone. I asked the friend to pass along the request to my colleague that he visit me the next evening. That was certainly bold, as the hospital is an hour's drive away and many people don't relish significant drives in November darkness to visit deeply ill people in locked wards. But, with the clear sense of purpose that informs someone trying to salvage important aspects of her life, I sent the message homeward. It's not as if the request was the first time I've significantly imposed on people when I've been ill.

My colleague arrived at the ward the next evening and, like all other visitors, was checked by the authorities for contraband. I had warned him in my message that he would have to endure that process. The list of prohibited items includes some you might not first think of, like cell phones, which are against the regulations because they could be used to take photos of people who might want to preserve their privacy as patients in the loony bin. The list of prohibited items naturally also includes knives and guns. And, as my minister was to find out on a different evening, even communion wine was not permitted into the ward, an excess of rigid regulations against alcohol, if ever there was one. I met my colleague by the nurses' station, where he gave me a bear hug.

Then, with the gift that locked wards inspired in people with the courage to make use of it, we fell into an intense conversation. I had anticipated talking about my job and when I hoped to get back to it. But we somehow barely mentioned that, instead discussing more important matters. Illness, death, and living, all were topics into which we delved.

My colleague was appalled to find I was just starting a potentially dangerous anti-seizure drug, but had no internet access to read the medical literature about the medication. I was quietly amused to find he was distressed, knowing much better than he how mental patients are all too often viewed by medical doctors, who think we cannot understand or evaluate our own treatment. We settled on the notion that my colleague would read up on the drug at home on the internet. That was a bit odd, perhaps, because he would have no easy way, from outside the hospital, to educate me about what he learned. But somehow that plan seemed to make him feel better, and thus me as well.

Although it may be difficult to enjoy an evening in a locked ward, I had as good and rich a time speaking with my colleague as could be hoped. When he had arrived, I would not have said I knew him on a personal level. When he left, I felt I had seen his true colors.

Once I was out of the hospital and had recovered enough to return to my office, I worked each day with the same good man who visited me in the locked ward. And as I mentioned to him when I first got back, I have not forgotten that evening. Although we veterans of mental hospitals can and do return to the ordinary backdrop of day-to-day life, busying ourselves with the ordinary, we never forget where we have been and who came to visit us while we were there.

As it happens, the psych unit nearest my hometown is in a Catholic hospital. I've met two Sisters working in the hospital over the years, both with the rare grace of being good listeners to people immersed in nothing short of hell. I think that the two nuns I've spoken with belong to that special – and small – sector of society composed of people who truly live out their values. That certainly makes them unlike me. But the good Sisters are similar to us psych patients in their willingness to talk about what really matters, including about life itself. So, in more than one way, I've been deeply inspired by the nuns, gladly and frequently recalling minding the grace they have shown me in the ward long after I've gone home.

Overall, I've benefited at several levels from my time in mental hospitals, especially because of my fellow patients and the nuns who gave us pastoral care. I don't think in-patient doctors or group meetings have ever helped me, except insofar as they are parts of the system that has kept me alive by limiting my freedom. But I know I'm a deeper citizen of the planet, richer both spiritually and psychologically, because of my sojourns on the inside of locked units.

All parts of a hospital, of course, have a natural intensity. The oncology unit is hardly a low-stress division of the institution, nor is the emergency room without a lot of strain. But what I term my part of the hospital is quite different and has much about it to be appreciated. For unlike all the other units in a hospital, where patients spend their days largely in isolation from one another in separate rooms, a psych ward is a community. We mental patients take our meals together, exercise with one another, and spend time together in group meetings. A psych ward thus creates a rare enclave where people from all backgrounds mix on close terms.

The ward is where I have learned a lot from people who hail from all walks of life, from business owners to welfare moms. The fact of community was brought home to me during that fall hospitalization when I wore ill-fitting clothes from the laundry closet so that I could wash the few items I had with me from home. The sweatpants and T-shirt I wore that afternoon united me with the homeless and others who had made use of them over time. Few places in our well-ordered society allow for the breaking down of socio-economic barriers, and those of us who have lived in the psych ward are, in that sense at a minimum, the better for it. Spending time with other patients who had quite different backgrounds from me greatly helped broaden my basic experience of life. My friendship with a woman around 30 years old named Mindy was one such aspect of life on the ward.

One afternoon I spent time with her as we both worked on a jigsaw puzzle on a table in the common room where we ate our meals. There were several puzzles available to us on the ward. Patients who were the most ill or drugged sometimes deliberately chose to work on puzzles made for children. With relatively few pieces, they could be put together in a single day even by the most impaired. Larger and more complex puzzles were available for the more able or ambitious.

Mindy and I labored together on one particular puzzle. She was a likeable woman a good bit younger than I was at age 50. She had short, dirty-blond hair, blue eyes, and a muscular build. Like most of us on the ward, she wore jeans, cargo pants, and T-shirts. She was married, with two kids in grade school.

Mindy's diagnosis was bipolar. Her medication list was even longer than mine, not a good sign about the strength of her illness. Just before coming to the hospital, she had quit a part-time job. She wanted to be as responsible as she could to her employer, and she had thought it better to walk in and resign than just leave in the night for the hospital or, as she put it, "be dead the next day." Monitoring our thoughts, evaluating how dangerous they are becoming, and trying hard to modify at least some of them were challenges that both Mindy and I shared. As she liked to say, "It's one thing to have birds sit on your head from time to time and shit on your hair." But it's another to let them build a nest up there without trying to scrape them off.

Although she had been ill all of her adult life, Mindy had several things going for her. She had a generous and thoughtful heart as evidenced by the fact that each day she went out of her way to thank the custodian who visited the psych ward to clean up after us. Mindy was also both a smart cookie and quite analytic. She had been through several quarters of community college and done well in math classes, excelling in calculus. That's not an accomplishment to be sneezed at anywhere in the country, and in her native rural Idaho, it set her clearly apart from most of her neighbors. Mindy was one of the very few patients in the ward who tumbled to the fact that I held a doctorate and had taught at the university level. She knew what that meant, even though it was clear she expected to remain in a working-class milieu all her life.

When Mindy was young, she had served time in jails in the northern panhandle of Idaho. As we labored over puzzle pieces, she explained that her local county jail served inmates simple bologna sandwiches each day for lunch, seven days a week.

"Two slices of bread, one slice of bologna, and a thin spread of mayo mixed with mustard. That was all we got for lunch, every day," she said.

By volunteering to work in the jail kitchen she had access to a bit more food as supper was prepared. But it was still clear that there hadn't been a great deal to eat for a young person with an active metabolism. Still, Mindy wasn't bitter about her time as a county guest, far from it. She thought it had been a difficult period but also a good one for her.

"Other inmates said they were innocent, and the world had ganged up on them and done them wrong," she said. "They never got past that. But somehow, I took the other attitude. I was guilty. I was the one who had screwed over my little part of the world."

Mindy's legal problems ended when she gave up using narcotics. That change was almost a decade in the past, so her status as clean was pretty well secured. Still, like many in the psych ward, she believed in regular attendance at "meetings," and was in fact in charge of a Narcotics Anonymous chapter in her hometown. Although I had plenty of experience with the abuse of alcohol decades earlier, I had quit by myself, never going to a twelve-step program. But my fellow patients often discussed Alcoholics Anonymous and Narcotics Anonymous and their differing philosophies about addiction and recovery. The difference between A.A. and N.A. was, in fact, the only abstract issue patients in the ward discussed. Still, whenever getting clean and sober came up for discussion, the psych ward patients with relevant experience could always agree that an addict was an addict no matter the drug of choice.

Mindy's husband and kids lived too far away to visit, but they called on the telephone several evenings. Her husband worked full-time but also had serious mental health issues and had been in a psychiatric hospital earlier in life. Mindy was clearly worried about how their kids would fare as they grew older. She talked about her fears with the openness that came so easily to most of us on the ward. Mindy's concern for her children clearly pained her more than her own suffering. No mother wants to think she and her husband have passed along the tendency for lifelong problems to their kids, and one of Mindy's young children had already been given a tentative diagnosis of major mental illness.

The choice to have children when you know you are chronically ill is a decision that can always be questioned. I had made my decision not to become a mother because I knew how deeply unwell I was and how tiny was the chance I could truly give all that's needed to young kids each day. But once children are on the scene, all a person can do is raise them as thoughtfully and responsibly as possible. For what it was worth, I assured Mindy she was, in fact, doing what she could for her children. She was setting a good example for them, living clean and sober and on the right side of the law, trying to get herself and her husband help from the doctors when they needed it, and working at a job whenever her health allowed. Nothing more, I said to Mindy, could be asked of her. And the downturn that had led her to flee to the protective custody of the psychiatric ward would soon, I hoped, be in the past. Mindy realized that my words were shaped with the best of intentions. But we also both knew we might each fare better when we got home – or we might spiral down into suicide. That was the long and the short of it, the bareboned facts of life for those with major mental health problems, the alums, if you will, of psych wards.

CHAPTER 7:

TRICKS OF THE TRADE

Anyone who successfully lives a life characterized by pain has tricks to help with coping. In the local hospital's psych ward, my friend Mindy shared my talent for getting away from problems through exercise. The two of us never missed the chance to work out in any fashion, walking together around the circular hallway of the ward, lap after lap, until others joked that we were wearing out the industrial carpet. And when we could, we made use of the small basketball room that lay outside the ward.

Mindy had an amazingly good shot from the far corner of the basketball room. It was a pleasure to watch my younger colleague size up the longest shot possible in the space we had and make it half of the time. She told me she had a hoop and backboard at home that her husband had put up for her as a birthday present some years previously. In northern Idaho's climate, outdoor basketball is possible in only a narrow slice of the year. But Mindy clearly had got in enough time on her home court that she had a great sense of the long shot.

Twenty years Mindy's senior and with a tricky shoulder, I had to be content to shoot from the general realm of the free-throw line, and I surely didn't hit .500. Still, that didn't matter. The point was to move and use our muscles. Dribbling and shooting during that hospitalization was one thing that liberated me from the worst of what I was feeling, lifting my spirits on even the darkest days. Exercise doesn't cure mental illness, of course, but there is some evidence that it helps brain chemistry run a little more evenly. Speaking as just one person locked inside a major mental illness, I can say that daily exercise helps me survive long enough to get through the dark of night and repeat the whole process of yet more exercise again the following day.

For more than 40 years now I've prescribed exercise to myself, and while it obviously doesn't make me well or even keep me out of hospitals, I am still alive. I think the biochemistry of working up a sweat is part of the reason for that basic fact. When we were escorted from the exercise rooms back to the regular section of the psych ward, I liked to tell the nurses and doctors how well Mindy and I had done on the court. I spun stories of games we had played against imaginary teams. The contests always came down to the final seconds, with Mindy taking a three-point shot, the buzzer sounding as the ball went through a perfect nothing-but-net swish.

"You should have been there!" I would wind up, flushed with genuine enthusiasm for the tale, just like I was ruddy from the exercise Mindy and I had shared. Quite honestly, in those moments I was puzzled the staff never played with us. They missed a great deal – but the normal people often do.

I only knew Mindy for a few days, but I came to respect her deeply. Because she was chronically ill, she showed the daily fortitude required to survive and function as best you can when you know you will never be well again. She was deeply dedicated to her kids and husband, and she did all she could to keep her hard-pressed family afloat financially. She was always alert to learning what she could from the psych ward staff, just as she had learned positive lessons from her time in jail. I could say that she deserved better cards than fate had dealt her, but perhaps it was because the cards she held were poor she had disciplined herself to do so much with so little.

Quite a few members of any psych ward community have been on the wrong side of the law at some point, especially when they were young. In some ways, I'm still a Sunday school girl, but I find breaking bread with most of the ex-cons in a mental hospital is perfectly agreeable. Apart from those with violent convictions and personalities to match, many of those who are veterans of jails are simple thieves and narcotic offenders who put away their transgressions easily enough when they gave up illegal drugs and started taking the kind the doctors prescribe.

My colleagues on the ward that fall who had been incarcerated in jails helped me understand the many rules imposed by the authorities on us psych patients. The internal logic of a locked ward is not so different from what keeps jails functioning on a daily basis. Except for common rooms like the dining area, two patients are never allowed in a room with a staff member, even if that means one patient stands in the hallway and waits to take a turn with the staffer after the first patient has left. The fear is that the patients, no matter how drugged or docile they may be, could attack the nurse or doctor using a two-to-one advantage. Nor can a patient walk into another patient's room, not even when a minister is visiting to hold a communion service. The fear is that if patients can go into one another's rooms, they will have sex – with each other, presumably, not the minister.

An amazing number of doors in a psych unit are locked. There are common areas, to be sure, but locked doors guard every other type of room, including the laundry room, interview rooms, and the all-important room where the drugs are kept. It takes a key to get through any door from either direction, meaning that even the highest-ranking psychiatrists must manage keys in their hands every few minutes throughout the day. The ward is run in this manner to secure the safety of the staff, the visitors, and perhaps even the patients. While my Ivy League education didn't explicitly prepare me to understand the ward's rules, I like to think all those years in school taught me a thing or two about learning. When my fellow patients with jail experience explained the rationale behind the rules, I quickly saw the reasons for the regulations. I learned something about myself and my common memories with my brother one Saturday when he visited the ward. When Nils arrived, I happened to be just launched onto a physical high.

To burn off energy, I wanted to move, so we walked briskly together around the circular hallway of the ward, passing patients and staff members alike. Our pace was quick, so much so that Nils shed layers of clothing down to his t-shirt. I was expansive and energetic, and our walk felt like we had been transported back to when we were kids and used to backpack with our parents in the mountains of the Northwest. As we walked around the hallway again and again, I could all but feel bright summer sun on my face and smell the scent of ponderosa pines. I almost jumped over a section of the dirty carpet near the nurses' station, taking it for a high mountain stream over which we were passing. Throughout that circular walk that seemed to stretch up a glaciated valley, I knew it was good to be alive, to be in my brother's company, and to re-experience viscerally what had been so intoxicating to me when we were young. It may be that Nils and I started to diverge from each other about the time we took those long-ago backpacking trips. There are times I imagine that we had similar joys up until the fire in my mind started to magnify normal pleasures almost to the point they cannot be borne. Another way of considering our different ways of living as adults is that perhaps Nils came down from the mountains where we used to hike. In contrast, I never have.

My endless alpine sojourn would explain why I can be transported back to high mountain meadows while walking in small circles around the narrow hallway of a psychiatric ward.

But the fire of my mind does not only dazzle with light. For as long as I have known it, the unusual blaze that flares up within me can project a sudden and dangerous darkness. The day after Nils visited me, I was compelled to visit dark depths. Lying in my hospital bed at dawn, I was pinned down by a black fog that materialized out of nowhere. In just a minute, intense pain pulled me down toward the finality of death. I felt the deep emotional grief of knowing I was to die and would never see Nils again.

Lying in that dark state for some time, my battered brain began to look forward to dying. Death would at least end the agony into which I had been dropped. If unbearable grief like that ever becomes aligned with action on my part, I know I won't live through the hour. It's not a question of giving up or lacking courage, and it's certainly not a matter of wanting to leave anyone I love. But like all fire, my internal blaze is dangerous. It's because of my first-hand experiences of the dark flames that I never condemn those who succumb to suicide. It's truly possible to see no other option but self-destruction. The vortex of death can be enormously stronger than a person. I'm starting to suspect Nils knows how close I've been to dying at the times I've been deeply ill. He may also suspect I'm smart enough to have figured out how to kill myself even in the hospital. Surely it takes real decency on his part to continue to relate to a sister who might someday take her own life.

My friends and others who care about me indeed have to shoulder the same burden. I know it's not a small matter for any of them. But for a brother, whose memories are intertwined with mine back to the earliest of long-ago times, the dangerous qualities of my internal life must sometimes be a heavy weight to carry.

Mind you, I generally do protect those close to me from the most extreme ideas that bounce around my brain. Usually, I say nothing about them to anyone. After all, I'm not really crazy. I know enough to realize it's to my advantage to get along with the throngs of normal people around me. And even when I let someone like my brother know what I am thinking, I try to limit the intensity I feel when I speak about my ideas. For example, despite all the emotion I could have put into my words when we walked together around the circular hallway of the psych ward, I think I spoke calmly to him about life-and-death issues.

That day in the hospital I explained to Nils that my doctor and I were arguing. I was determined not to take another drug in the family known as atypical antipsychotics, while the psychiatrist wanted me to give another one a whirl. I've always thought that atypical antipsychotic drugs have a name that's tough to spin. But it's not the label attached to the drugs that I object to. I felt, and still believe, that quitting the tremor-inducing drug ultimately led to suffering that came close to killing me that fall. I explained to Nils while we walked that I was indeed quite ill. In my best matter-of-fact tone, I said that when I got out of the hospital, I wasn't sure if I would make it through the winter. But I was determined to live or die at home, with the illness I knew so well, and with only drugs that had effects I could best predict. Hence, I said to Nils, no more atypical antipsychotics.

Nils didn't argue with me about the drugs. But my doctor used every trick in the book while I was in the locked ward to try to get me to take another atypical antipsychotic. He pleaded with me to do so on some days, criticizing me testily on many others. But I didn't give in. In sum, I think there are times it can be better to die on your own terms than try to live on your doctor's.

Toward the end of that increasingly miserable hospitalization, I descended into full psychosis. A long time after Mindy had gone home, I was alone in the basketball room, trying desperately to combat the dark surges in my mind with some exercise. Then, I experienced the host of wonderful and magical people sitting in bleachers beyond a sheetrock wall, all cheering me on. During the dark winter at home, I recalled the magical people to mind every night when I went to bed. I longed to be back in their presence, to simply be with them as I had during those remarkable exercise periods. I'm not sure, but perhaps the good Lord can use psychosis to give a deeply ill person what she needs to continue. All I really know is that the magical people of the basketball room were the most important feature of that long hospitalization and in some ways the most important feature of my whole life.

For me, one of the toughest aspects of living is that I now know the full drill of what having my mental disorder is like. My illness is a series of unpredictable and demanding events, a never-ending cycle of states and episodes outside the ordinary, most of which are deeply painful and some of which are life-threatening. When you understand the illness and all it entails, you can't deny the fact that part of the disease is made of cycles that repeat.

Downs follow ups, rattlesnakes are followed by angels. The upside to the fact that part of the disease is cyclic, is that when I stagger into a locked ward, I have strong reason to hope I'll walk back out of it. But the problem with recovery is that the whole cycle is starting anew, which means I'll later become ill again. And throughout it all, whether I'm up, down, or sideways, I cannot forget my worst experiences.

If you have high energy levels that sometimes mark mental illness, a psych ward's natural intensity is quite welcome. For one thing, conversations about life and death come easily in such settings, partly because many people are considering suicide. At two o'clock in the afternoon and two o'clock in the morning, there's bound to be someone just as worked up as you are, ready to talk about the abyss nearby. Thus, I sometimes spend hours with my counterparts discussing whether we should accelerate the final end of our illness by making a deal with the dark angel we must all meet at some point anyway.

But no matter how manic, depressed, or mixed I may be, there are moods in which suicide just isn't my cup of tea. Happily, there are other interesting conversations in any psych ward worth its salt. At some point during the day, some patients will spontaneously gather around a table and turn the conversation toward a topic like what life is like in jails. Or we might discuss the strong side-effects of heavy-duty psychiatric medications. Then there are the remarkable peculiarities of many psychiatrists. And always there is the problem of addiction and the daily struggle to live clean and sober.

When I'm on the inside, I make good use of my days on the ward by talking intensely for an hour with my fellow patients, then pacing in the hallways as I turn matters over in my mind. At times my thinking runs in tight little circles, periods I literally cannot think straight. But even then, I have found that I can generally evaluate what I've heard with a couple hours of pacing. Then I rest my arthritic knees by sitting down to join the next interesting conversation.

There were some other interesting elements about that November stay in the hospital. One set of my experiences revolved around – of all things – poetry. During that long sojourn in the institution, I often found myself reciting all the poetry I knew by heart. Day after day, poems came to mind unbidden. I have more scripture memorized than secular verse, but it must have been the sector of my brain that stores English poetry that was activated by illness or drugs. Over a few days, every scrap of poetry I know came to me, whether I wanted to think of them or not. I silently quoted poems to myself as I walked the circular hallway of the ward and quoted them aloud most days to the psychiatrist when he came to see me. The short, blazingly manic poems of Edna St. Vincent Millay were appropriate, of course, and I reveled in them. Emily Dickenson and small fragments of Shakespeare also came to mind.

Although I know a few poems and a good bit of scripture by heart, it's not often in normal life that I quote them. Geologists live and think in prose, not poetry nor sacred text. We are a mundane lot in that respect, even those of us who are exotic enough to be crazy. Even at my worst, when illness distorts the basic framework of my mind, I never dream of writing poetry. Some parts of the human brain are perhaps missing in geologists, and making rhyme and meter work together has always been well beyond my talents.

As it happened, my psychiatrist wrote poetry at the time of the November hospitalization. He had told me so when I was an outpatient. At one point he had told me he wanted to learn the basic geologic setting of the soil around his house because he was writing a poem about gardening. He asked me about the local geology and how the soil had been formed. I may have thought the question a bit odd, but I supplied the information, which was easy enough to do.

On the day I was to get out of the locked ward my psychiatrist appeared for our last meeting. As doctors do at such times, he was sizing me up for suicidal tendencies, trying to estimate how well or badly things were going. As patients do at such times, I was trying to get a clearer framework for moving into the broader world after my time in the institution. I can't speak for the doctor, but I know I felt I didn't get what I wanted. I had been so unwell in the fall, and ill in a different pattern than ever before in my life, I had worn myself out thinking about what might have contributed to the tsunami of autumn suffering. Were my life-threatening symptoms some delayed effects of the drugs the doctor had changed during the summer, or was my biological illness simply worsening horribly and quickly? In a rush, I made a mental leap to something that seemed to capture part of what was bothering me about all I didn't know.

"What aren't you telling me?" I intensely queried the doctor across the tiny interview room.

He almost jumped from his chair, swinging his hand over to his chest and hitting the front of his suitcoat.

"Me?" he retorted. "Nothing!"

Either the psychiatrist was a great actor, or he really had told me what he knew. Our conversation then turned to a couple of less intense topics. When I thought the interview was over, the doctor turned to his briefcase. He withdrew a single piece of paper on which a short poem he had written was printed. He gave the sheet to me.

As a polite woman, I certainly knew I should thank him for the gift, and I did so. And, in some ways, I was flattered to receive it. After all, I doubted he gave his poetry to other patients, so many of whom were poorly educated in rural and impoverished North Idaho. But as I folded the paper and put it in my back pocket, I also felt uneasy about what had just happened. Would the doctor ask me to respond to the poem in some way at our next appointment in the outpatient clinic? Did I have to find something positive to say about it to remain in his good graces? Writers can be plenty touchy about their words. I know that through many years of experience with myself.

My minister says the psychiatrist strayed over professional lines in giving me anything so personal as a poem while I was locked up. She may be right. But I've given my own writing to so many people for so many decades that the matter doesn't seem so significant to me as it does to her. Once I recovered from the hospital, I had the internal strength not to feel threatened by the poem. But it was odd to get such a personal gift from someone in authority in a locked ward. Looking back, I'd say the poem was a blurring of boundaries and it was good for the minister to be concerned. I was discharged from the hospital in late November, two weeks after entering it. I had lost weight and strength, and, as luck would have it, I was discharged into freshly falling snow. Leaving any hospital is emotional, and leaving a locked ward has its own emotional burdens. I was glad to go, but also afraid of how very ill I still was and what might become of me away from the safety of the ward.

My sister-in-law's mother gave me a ride back to my hometown through the weather rapidly deteriorating into a major snowstorm. After I got home, I greeted my elderly mother who lived with me, and my dog Buster Brown, a large and faithful mutt originally from the pound.

Greetings done, I sat down with a cup of tea and took stock of myself. The most impressive thing to me that afternoon was the realization that I was thoroughly depleted. I had been institutionalized for a long time that fall, in two lengthy periods quite close together, and those episodes had knocked me down and pummeled me. I'd lost about 10 percent of my weight and a great deal more of my strength and stamina. I'm sure it didn't help that the late-November weather into which I was released was unusually frigid – a condition that doesn't make life any easier even when you're well.

The first evening I was home, all I did was lie on the sofa in front of the small woodstove that's squeezed into a corner of the modest living room of my home. The next morning it didn't look like I could do much more than again lie around. But then a mild surge of manic energy washed over me. Recognizing I had a window of time to function, I decided how to take advantage of the upswing that was beginning to course through my body.

Quickly, I got into my flannel-lined jeans, heavy jacket, leather boots, and wool mittens. With my warmest goose-down hat pulled down around my head and neck, I went outside into 14-degree weather. Wading in the deep snow, I dug my 23-year-old Ford pickup out of a substantial snowdrift. I had known I wouldn't have much time to work before I started to lose energy, and that was certainly the case. As my strength waned away, I quickly slipped onto the bench seat of the stone-cold truck.

Remarkably enough on that bitter morning, the engine of the old brown Ford turned over, cranked a while, and then fully roared to life. The torque from the engine gave a satisfying twist to the vehicle frame as the engine surged and raced. I left it running so it could warm up and slowly slogged through the snow to go inside my house.

When my fingers were finally warm and more flexible, I called a friend who had no vehicle but needed to get to work to feed the many mouths in his family. Over the phone I explained to him I had an old but functioning truck I could loan him. A couple days later I changed my mind about the loan and simply signed the vehicle's title over to him, a decision vindicated by his exuberant joy. As I like to say, there's no point in being manic if you don't know how to use it.

Episodes of energy, activity, and quick decisions have long made up my life. And there have been deeper surges that have rocketed me into greater projects of all sorts. I've written more than half a dozen books, quit as many Jobs, found new employment, earned a doctorate in natural science from Harvard, joined quite different religious denominations, taken up with men, broken up with same, and bought a couple of houses.

Most gloriously of all, I purchased a beautifully restored red and white 1967 motorboat for which I had no clear purpose. I think all these events and accomplishments have been made possible by the intense internal energy I also suspect fuels the rattlesnakes and auditory hallucinations with which I live. The valuable parts of the energy surges are one reason I suspect I don't really want to be cured of the bipolar states that characterize my kind of schizoaffective disorder. The doctors can say what they wish, but I value digging a beloved truck out of the snow when I really had no business doing more than eating chicken soup. Or as I put it to myself some days, what if I lacked the risk-taking tendencies that stand behind my decisions over the years to quit safe jobs for the challenge of starting over in new fields? Honestly, I respect the normal people around me. But leading a predictable life most folks do hardly looks exciting.

I was discharged on Monday of the week of Thanksgiving. It was a long and miserable week, spent snow-bound inside my house day after day. Thanksgiving Day was the same as the others had been. My mother and I spent the day indoors, looking at the mounds of snow all around us. We ate spaghetti because that's what we had on hand. But I was indeed thankful. I was thankful to be out of the hospital, thankful to be getting five hours of sleep per night rather than three, and thankful that despite the uncertainties of cosmic cost-benefit analyses, society had invested in me once more.

In the hospital, I had lost the ability to concentrate and even to read more than a few minutes. It was absolutely stupefying to be so mentally blunted I couldn't read, but such was the case. Throughout that first week at home, I still could barely concentrate enough to write out a few simple checks to pay my most pressing bills. It felt like I simply couldn't gather my thoughts enough to make the act of check-writing possible.

My severe stupidity, very likely, was the effect of the anti-seizure drugs or the medication changes the doctors had made in the hospital. To be sure, each day I tried to read. But after 5 minutes of effort, I would be defeated. But on Friday night of my first week home, I managed to read the forward to a book by Mark Vonnegut, Kurt Vonnegut's son. The book detailed Mark's significant mental illness but also his ability to work as a pediatrician despite his problems. I was exhausted by the effort, but I also noted that I had read more than in the past and felt more hopeful.

The next morning, I started to read right after breakfast. I made slow progress through the pages of the book's first chapter, but I was able to keep reading until mid-morning. The pleasure I took in being able to read for a couple of hours was almost magical. After some mid-morning coffee, I sat down again with the book. Bit by bit, reading became easier. By noon I was doing better still. I continued to read well into the afternoon. Finally, by the end of the day, I could read in my normal adult fashion, concentrating sufficiently without difficulty. In a mere 24-hours I had regained the ability to read, a clear sign my brain was recovering from the worst of what had been ailing it. I staggered from November to December that fall, much too ill to work. My days were spent at home talking to my mother or outside, walking my dog. At first, I walked just around the neighborhood, then further around more of the small town I call home. Soon, however, I drove down to the bottom of the Snake River Canyon where I walked for miles along the railroad tracks, far from any road so the dog could be off-leash.

The first day along the river wasn't easy. I had spent time in the hospital considering committing suicide by throwing myself off the canyon's cliffs, so being in their presence created deep emotional challenges. Besides that, I was weakened from the two long hospital stays, and I felt significant strain during the last couple miles of my walk on the railroad tracks, almost stumbling forward, step after step. But the second time I left the plateau where I live and went down to the Snake, I ambled easily and well along the river. After that, there was no looking back, and I walked six miles on the railroad tracks for quite a number of days. I honestly thought all my walking was voluntary, not compulsive. But in the days that followed I had to admit I had deeply bruised three toenails and given myself blisters. Nothing significant was lost, however: only one toenail came out entirely, and as usual, the good Lord came through with a new one growing up where the old one had been.

When I was a graduate student in Cambridge the main risk during my long compulsive walks were that I'd be mugged, raped, or murdered. I suppose at home there's a tiny risk I'll meet some man in the empty canyons and coulees where I amble, someone who will do me wrong when literally no one is within miles of us. But I think I face a slightly greater threat to my safety from wildlife. I saw a cougar once in the Snake River Canyon, sitting on his butt in the snow that had come halfway down the canyon walls on that January day. Cougars routinely kill sheep in and near the canyon. They have been known to attack women joggers in the rural Northwest, presumably choosing us females because we're smaller than our male counterparts and thus easier to bring down. It's selfish, to be sure, but I like to hope any cougar I meet may go for my dog rather than me. I'd deeply grieve the loss of my Lab mix, but in most of my ever-changing moods I also want to live another year or two, not just turn into a meal for a cougar.

Although I regained some physical strength that December, the demons of my mind still tormented me, and I was far too ill to work. I slept little and didn't eat enough to regain the weight I had lost in the hospital. Toward Christmas I reluctantly concluded I must try another atypical antipsychotic drug. I had resisted such drugs while I was institutionalized, but the several drugs I was on were not restoring me to health sufficiently so I could work for a living. I simply had to have income and trying an atypical antipsychotic seemed like it might help me get back to work. I talked to my psychiatrist who was glad of this change of heart on my part. He prescribed a newer antipsychotic, and I tried it for several days. Within 72 hours I was a clear step better, and I felt great relief to have found something that helped. But a day after that I developed a strong tremor in my hands – exactly the symptom that had led the doctor during the previous summer to have me quit the antipsychotic I was then taking.

Consulting with the psychiatrist by phone, he indicated that, given the tremor, he didn't want me to continue with the drug. Neither did I. So, it seemed we were back to Square One with a long and dark winter still looming over me.

Even being charitable to the doctors and the drug companies, it's fair to say the treatment for serious mental illness is a mixed bag. The side effects of psych drugs are often substantial and often start the first day you take the medications. Potential benefits are experienced only down-the-road and may be obtained only at such high doses of the drug that the side effects are crippling. Over the years I've tried more than twenty psychiatric medicines. Looking back at all my experiences with the drugs, I feel qualified to say that neither major mental illness nor the treatment for it is for sissies.

But there's also little choice but to try the meds. Some of them, at least in some ways, can help an individual. When your back is against the wall, as is the case for the seriously mentally ill, you look for help wherever you can find it. Thus, those of us with major mental illness try medication after medication, putting up with strong side effects in the hope of finding some relief from the disease. I have yet to find a drug that eases all my symptoms – witness the fact there are still rattlesnakes around my feet at times, I hear encoded messages in common sounds from time to time, and I cycle back into the locked ward occasionally. But the meds do help me to some degree. So, I swallow them, often several at a time, each and every day. And I live with the hope that some new drug will reach the market that will help the ill still more and perhaps harm us less.

But as the New Year dawned, I was still depressed and violent visions of death still plagued me. My mind might work more normally for a few hours, but then I would be enveloped in a dense and dark fog. Rattlesnakes swarmed on the floor. One afternoon I saw the face of death, wearing a dark mask, just a few inches in front of my eyes. I turned my head to the right to try to escape the image, but it followed me. I turned to the left with no better result. I put my hands over my eyes and found a small measure of relief. But there was no doubting I was still very ill. I didn't think about what it would cost to go to the hospital when I twice did so that fall. I was quite manic and at the end of my rope during October. Then, in November, I was suddenly and significantly depressed and suicidal. In short, I was desperate and not in a position to run careful cost-benefit analyses regarding in-patient care.

When I'd been home for a month, I started to be a bit bothered that I had not seen a bill for either of my hospital stays. In my lighter moods I wondered if my sojourns in the psychiatric ward were free. Perhaps that was part of President Obama's health care package I didn't grasp when he signed it into law. How wonderful that crazy people should stay in hospitals without charge.

When I felt more sober, I wondered if society had ever done a cost-benefit analysis on my life. After all, I have had recurring periods of illness when I can't work and am all but past praying for. It was well and good for the deep-pockets of Harvard University to pay for my countless hospitalizations in graduate school. But in my 30s, I was hospitalized for ten days in the rural Northwest when I had no significant income or insurance. Only that last resort of the poor, our nation's odd patchwork of government-provided medicine, was around to foot the bill.

Going to a mental hospital without insurance or resources is a bit like being a hiker lost in the mountains. Sometimes society does a great deal in an effort to save your life. Search parties are organized, helicopters fly low over the trees, and hounds are set loose on a scent trail. Similarly, sometimes us suicidal citizens get the finest of responses from our neighbors. Even without the ability to pay, we are packed off to endure the worst of what our demons can do in the relative safety of a locked ward. It's amazing to experience a positive and generous response from society, in particular when you are sure you are not worth the trouble.

While I waited for the hospital bills in the winter of 2011, I told myself not to worry about what I might owe. After all, this time I had a full-time job and good insurance to match. But, then again, I had just missed three months at work. Pretty much everything felt exceedingly fragile, including my ability to pay the hospital.

But basic medical issues were more pressing than thoughts about hospital charges. Trying to make some change that could help me, I suggested to the psychiatrist that we try the antipsychotic my friend Mindy in the hospital had been on, a drug called Zyprexa. There was no really good reason to try that particular antipsychotic, but the doctor was as comfortable giving me an antipsychotic I was actually asking for as he was just picking one off the list of such medications. So it was that I started Zyprexa. After a week on the medication, I was sleeping much better, and, to my relief, I had not developed a tremor. I continued to take Zyprexa and returned to part-time work. Encouraged that I could function at least a bit, I ate more, slept more deeply, and soon returned to full-time work. I had missed about three months at my job but as January dissolved into February, I could take comfort in the idea I was back in the saddle again.

The university job I returned to was as demanding as when I had left it. Editing grant proposals measured in the millions of dollars required me to be sharp and highly focused. Working with the faculty members in charge of the proposals sometimes required diplomacy, as it fell to me to remind them of internal deadlines and the need to stay on top of the multi-faceted work every step of the way. At times I had to correct faculty's understanding of the government's rules or the specific requirements of the competitions for which the proposals were to be submitted. The proposals themselves sometimes hinged on abstract science such as modern genetics or biochemistry. In short, the job was a difficult and demanding one. In several ways I enjoyed all I did at the university, but as I got back to work that winter and spring, I started to notice something that bothered me deeply. When I was younger, I retained even abstract and difficult material. But gnawing at my consciousness now was the understanding that I wasn't making long-term memories of what I learned from the grant proposals I was editing. My memory was slipping. That notion was frightening, and it took courage even to think it over. I examined the idea several times and was forced to the same conclusion: the gears of my mind were starting to slip when it came to learning difficult material of the sort I had loved when I was young. I was scared about what seemed to be happening, and I complained to the psychiatrist that I couldn't think as well and remember as much as I was used to. The doctor dismissed my concerns.

"You're an absent-minded Ph.D.," he said to me in his office. "That's your problem."

It was true that I had always been a bit absentminded about such things as where my reading glasses might be. Truth be known, sometimes I found them on top of my head after futilely searching my desk for them. But that wasn't the issue that bothered me now. My concern was that I was no longer a sharp cookie, that I wasn't digesting and learning the science I was reading at work. I tried again to explain that to the psychiatrist, but he refused to take me seriously.

"Your intellectual self-confidence may be shaken because you were ill," he said, "but you're my brightest patient."

I am vain enough I was flattered by the doctor's words, but I also realized we were in a stalemate. I was sure something was wrong, but the doctor was equally certain things were fine. I could see no help for it but for me to keep my counsel on the matter and hope for the best. Maybe all I was noticing was the effect of simple aging. Perhaps this was what it felt like to have turned 50 years old? Then again, my memory problems might be part of my mental illness. I just didn't know and the psychiatrist was no help.

There was also no help for my limited social life. Around the time I spoke to the psychiatrist, I started to go out with an electrical engineer I knew from town. Ethan was a good-looking blonde, a low-key guy who worked at a high-tech firm in the area. I enjoyed the fact that he wasn't caught up in university life but spent his working days in an entirely different milieu. We went on Sunday afternoon walks together, and talked over coffee. I had hopes for us, as we seemed to like a number of the same things and we enjoyed each other's company. But the day came when I told Ethan I had been diagnosed with bipolar disorder. We were facing each other in a coffee shop when I outlined what the illness meant for me. Ethan's eyes narrowed as he took in the news. I suspected things were not going well because he didn't want to talk about mental illness, or what my diagnosis really meant. Instead, he changed the subject to another matter entirely. Sure enough, he never called me again.

Earlier in life, I didn't face the question of what to tell a man about my problems which were then ill-defined. I was terribly ill, but I just let the men find that out for themselves. But in middle age, I have been given a clear diagnosis. It seems only right to tell my friends a fact that's so important to who I am. But that also scares off some men with whom I'd like to spend more time. Such was the case with Ethan.

But I don't blame someone who doesn't want to become involved with someone strongly ill. I've often thought I wouldn't live with myself if I had any say. It's not easy for anyone to deal with an insomniac who dances into mental difficulties. In that way, I wish I were well, and I understand a man's reluctance to become involved with a woman who is strongly unwell. Still, Ethan's rejection stung.

After I had put the psych ward firmly behind me, and successfully returned to work, the time came for me to start laboring once more on the climate change manuscript that had been on my desk for a long time. When I had fallen ill I had been in mid-stream of the rewrite effort. Settling back into weekend work on the manuscript, I soldiered onward, trying to tell the tale of how scientists had learned of massive and repeated climate change. I emailed my literary agent, saying that I would soon be finished. He requested me to add a chapter about the evidence of tree rings and climate change. The subject was easy enough for readers to understand, and I was glad to make it part of the book. I was interested in ending the book with something other than a summary, preferably with some new material that would interest and surprise people. I had exactly that topic about which geologists know but which non-geologists are generally unaware. It's a simple fact that the Earth's coal, both above ground and underground, is on fire in many places around the world. Coal fires are a bit like forest fires, except they are not seasonal.

In the U.S. they burn in rural places, such as the Appalachians, the West, and Alaska. Many coal fires burn in ancient coalfields, such as in China. Massive coal fires burn in India, with flames leaping into the sky from coal seams at the surface. Some coal fires are ignited by slash-and-burn agriculture, some by coal mining accidents. It's not easy to say exactly how much carbon dioxide is produced by unwanted coal fires. For example, it's impossible to precisely say how much a particular underground fire is burning at a given time. But some estimates indicate that if all coal fires were extinguished the world around, we could eliminate as much carbon dioxide as American cars spew forth each year. It seems elementary that if we are seriously concerned about greenhouse gases, we should invest the funds needed to put out coal fires.

With coal fires as one of the major points in my final chapter, I felt the climate manuscript was complete. I sent the electronic files to my agent, who started peddling the manuscript around New York. That effort stretched over a couple of months. In the end, a small but serious press – Prometheus Books – agreed to publish it. The advance they offered worked out to be much less than the minimum wage considering all the time I had put into the book. Still, I was glad to have a publisher. Mostly I rejoiced because once published, the book would be done and I could go on to something else.

Less than a year had passed between when I'd been released from the psych ward and when I'd finished the climate manuscript. For weeks after getting out of the hospital I had been laid low by my depression. Rattlesnakes and the face of death appeared before me at random intervals. So, it could be considered surprising I'd been able to do as much as I had on the book that year. But, in the odd world in which I live, rapid recoveries are just as possible as rapid descents into major illness. It's impossible to say how much of my recovery was due to medications, and how much to some random biochemical change within my brain. Of course, I was grateful for it, and I remember being quietly glad I had lived long enough to finish the climate manuscript. In my world, staying alive is not to be taken for granted.

After the climate book came out, my religious life took an interesting turn. As it happens, a women's Benedictine monastery is about two hours south of my hometown. I don't remember quite how it happened, but through church connections, I ended up on the Monastery of St. Gertrude mailing list. One day I read in the monastery's newsletter about a special program the sisters were offering for writers and artists to spend time living at the monastery. I applied for the program. My literary agent and my minister wrote me letters of recommendation, an interesting pairing if ever there was one.

To my delight, I was accepted to the program and was able to schedule two weeks of vacation from work so that I could go. I bought a copy of The Rule of Benedict, the document written by St. Benedict many centuries ago about how he thought monastic life should be ordered. Soon I was packing my suitcase to be a guest of the sisters and experience something of their world. I wasn't sure what to expect, both in the simple day-to-day sense of what life in a monastery is like and what daily structured prayer might do to my spirits and my psychiatric states. But it seemed clear to me I would likely only have one chance in life to experience a Benedictine monastery, and whatever the costs might be, I wanted to go.

The Monastery of St. Gertrude is situated at the foot of a wooded ridge outside the small town of Cottonwood, Idaho. The main building houses both the place of worship for the community and the nuns' rooms. I was given such a room, a simple and narrow space with a sink near the door and a window at the head of the twin bed. Because it was August and quite hot, I was issued a fan that I put in the window to blow outside air inwards into the room. Meals were taken at scheduled times in a large and sunny dining room on the first floor of the building. The grounds around the building were simple but pleasant. A large lawn lay in front of the building. It was watered enough to keep it mostly green. Behind the building were two things: a graveyard where Benedictine nuns were laid to rest and a trail that led through the woods up the ridge.

The monastery's dining room and living quarters were larger than the modern community needed. Like other orders, the Benedictines in the U.S. face dwindling numbers. Perhaps because women now have a number of options in the working world, fewer and fewer women are joining houses like St. Gertrude. While I was there, the community prayed for new members and invited women to visit, but only one young nun had recently joined. Most of the sisters were in their 70s or beyond.

Everyone in a monastery has a job, even the frail and elderly who may only have the assignment of prayer. My job while I resided at St. Gertrude was to work on my writing. At the time I was finishing up the proof pages of the climate change manuscript. My efforts were scheduled to be published that fall under the title The Whole Story of Climate. A Sister gave me a small office in which to work, and I labored on the book one last time. In the evenings I wrote a few chapters of a children's story for a change of pace. That, plus worship three times per day, was how my time was structured.

Before landing at St. Gertrude, I had been concerned that a strong change of pace might cause me psychiatric problems. I talked the matter over with my psychiatrist. The doctor and I developed an outline of how I could increase the dosage of my medications if I began to experience problems at the monastery. I also talked about the same issues with my mother. We agreed I could call her each evening and report on how things were going in my head and what it was like to be a daily part of St. Gertrude.

Although I was concerned about how the monastic life might affect my psychiatric symptoms, I also had high hopes that regular prayers and a disciplined life might lead me to mystical experiences. To give myself options depending on what happened, I packed my whole arsenal of medicines to take with me. Perhaps because I was taking a lot of bipolar medications, I experienced no mystical trips while I stayed with the sisters. That was a disappointment. But on the good side, I didn't experience strong illness or psychotic breaks when I was at the monastery. I enjoyed my time with the sisters.

My one significant disappointment concerned the middle-aged nun whom I had met in the psychiatric ward during my stay at the Catholic hospital years previously. She was a member of St. Gertrude but didn't return to the monastery while I was there. She was, I was told, all too often busy with her job in the hospital in the city, rarely visiting her home base. I was sorry I didn't get a chance to speak with her, in particular, because she had made such a positive impression on me when I was at my worst in the locked ward of the hospital. But talking with other Sisters about everything under the sun was both educational and interesting.

I was not alone in my status as a visitor at the monastery. Three other women, all younger than I was, were also making sojourns at the institution. We four tended to eat together, and as the days went by we shared the story of our lives. One of the three was considering whether she had a vocation to join an order. She was from Philadelphia and had a mild accent I had seldom heard since leaving the East Coast. She had been raised a Catholic and knew her way around all the services. She fasted each Thursday to show her concern for a child she knew who was dealing with cancer. Of course, she also prayed for that child and a host of other issues ranging from peace in Afghanistan to much more trivial matters in personal life. It seemed to me she did have a vocation, and one day I told her so. She visibly brightened. In the end, it would require a lot of prayer and reflection to determine whether she truly belonged as a monastic. In that sense, her time at St. Gertrude was just the first step on a long journey.

I finished the final touches of the climate manuscript while I was at the monastery. I emailed the last section to New York using the internet connection there. A few months later, in November of 2012, the book came out. A friend of mine set up a website for the book for promotional purposes and with the help of a teenage neighbor I made a short video for the website. With no budget for travel, I did a few book signings in my hometown and Spokane, Washington, a couple of hours away by car. The book got some good reviews in newspapers, but it did not sell enough to matter. To soothe my ego, my agent told me it was nevertheless a significant book. And I had the satisfaction of feeling I had done my best to make the public aware of the complexities of natural climate change.

The next change I had to consider was quite personal. The death of my elderly father taught me something about what mental illness and grief have in common, as well as what makes them different. The events of that time started on a Saturday morning when my brother called to say our father had experienced a heart attack. I was out walking my dog on a long trek, so it took me time to get home, put the dog in the house, and go to the Assisted Living facility where my father was residing.

Nils told me that Papa's blood pressure values had been very low when he arrived on the scene first thing in the morning, but since then they had largely recovered. By early afternoon, and with morphine in his system to control chest pain, Papa sat up in bed and made a few jokes. Sometime later, after another round of morphine, my brother got my father up and into his wheelchair. We all then sat outside in the warmth of an August afternoon, enjoying the pleasant day and the shade made by the building.

My sister-in-law and niece joined us, completing the family circle. We talked of various ordinary matters. My father spoke hardly at all, but he was part of the group and listened to what we were saying. His wife of more than 65 years was there with him. In time he asked to be wheeled back indoors. As my brother got Papa back to his room, he suffered another heart attack and became unresponsive. Once he was transferred to his bed, unconscious, it became clear to us that he was dying.

Throughout the day I had felt the intensity of the events that were unfolding. I spent a bit of time monitoring my internal states, a habit of those of us who have known great mental illness for a long time. Although I had felt a lot of stress as soon as I got my brother's phone call, I also had noted that there were no rattlesnakes around me as the day unfolded. That changed with my father's second heart attack. Once we openly spoke of an impending death, the rattlesnakes appeared on my father's room floor. Late in the afternoon, my unconscious father's breathing became more and more labored. I had a strong desire to get my feet up off the floor, away from the snakes. That simply wasn't possible. At my age, with my stiff and painful knees, I couldn't sit cross-legged on a chair as I did when I was in my 20s. I knew the rattlers would be plaguing me for at least the rest of the day and into the night. Because I had never experienced the death of a parent before, I wondered what other tricks my mind might play as I went through a major loss.

My father never regained consciousness and he died that evening. I kissed him on the forehead and tried to do what I could to comfort my mother. As we sat for a time with the body, I constructed my first reflections on all that he had meant to me over half a century. He had created a home with my mother into which I was born and had an active role in rearing me. My love of learning partly came from his example of intellectual life as a long-time faculty member.

Because I have been so ill so much of my adult life, he has been important to me as someone who always stood ready to help me. When I stumbled away from Harvard, an underweight and fully tormented 30-year-old, I had fled to his household where he took me in. Because he and my mother took such good care of me, I had lived through the worst things my mind could generate. And even long after that, as episodes of illness conspired to lay me low again and again, my father had been there for me. I had lost a great deal with his passing. I took stock of the fact that I had to go home where I knew I might face a difficult night. Even normal people feel a lot of grief when there is a death in the family.

I would have to face the first stage of my loss, while also dealing with the rattlesnakes that were close to my feet.

When I got home, I took what was then my usual bedtime psychiatric drugs – three different pills – and then another three medicines that are optional medicines I can use to try to slow down my brain. I rarely take the three optional meds together. But this was a night to pull out all the stops. I crawled into bed, saying a prayer for my dead father and one for myself. Under the influence of six significant and sedating psychiatric medicines, I was able to sleep fitfully most of the night.

My employer automatically granted me a week's bereavement leave, and I was interested to note that even though my father had been old and ill when he died, I truly needed that week off. It wasn't that I was sitting around crying; indeed, I hardly wept at all. But my thoughts were often high-jacked by memories of my father. I would be sitting at the breakfast table, reading the newspaper, when some small thing my father had said to me twenty years previously would intrude into my mind. Or, driving across town, I would remember it was my father who had taught me how to drive, even before I was old enough to have a learner's permit legally. The memories were not unpleasant in any way, but I couldn't turn them off. In that way, grief had something important in common with mental illness. In the midst of illness and hospitalizations, I can't control my thoughts, which may center on suicidal ideas, the presence of the rattlesnakes, or obsessions about small matters. Like those experiences of illness, journeying through grief made parts of my thinking involuntary.

But memories of my father didn't pain me like mental illness can. And once I accepted that I would simply have to experience the recollections when they washed over me, I got through the week without major psychiatric difficulties. But it was also true that I had a strange sensation in my chest one day early in the week. It was a little like one of the physical symptoms of depression with which I am well familiar, but it was also clearly different. It took me a while to realize that it felt like my heart was heavy. I then understood the origin of the English phrase "a heavy heart." As the week unfolded, I found I didn't have the physical energy to swim, but I walked the dog long distances each day. By the end of the week, I was a couple of pounds lighter and had two blisters on my feet, but I didn't think I was manic. Grief had simply led to hours of walking each day without enough eating to offset the calories burned.

Being with my father on his last day made for a change in my attitude about death. Simply put, I became much less afraid of death than I was before he passed. I still fear the suffering that can come before the final moments of life, and I think I fear the fact that we don't know what death or any afterlife may be like. But the dying process is much less distressful to me than it was. That is quite a gift my father's death gave me, one I truly treasure and hope to retain as I move forward into the later stages of my own life.

CHAPTER 8:

FINAL DIAGNOSIS

The time came when my aging psychiatrist retired from medical practice. He handed me off for care to a younger doctor. I was a bit nervous about the change, but I had to hope for the best. When I met Dr. Jamie Rambeau, she made a good impression. A trim woman, she was younger than I but not so young as to be inexperienced. She carefully took my history, paying particular attention to the medications I had tried over the years. We talked about some of the problems I had had since I was young. I'm sure she asked me if I heard voices, and I'm equally sure I denied such symptoms. I didn't want to admit – to myself or anyone else – that I did in fact have auditory hallucinations. From listening to others in the psychiatric ward, I was quite sure that acknowledging that I heard strange things would make my diagnosis and prognosis worse, and I didn't have what it took to face that.

When we had gotten to know each other a bit, I complained to Dr. Rambeau about my cognitive problems. She took me much more seriously than her predecessor and didn't dismiss my concerns. Indeed, she sent me for all-day testing by a neuropsychologist. The exam consisted of many mental and memory tests, ranging from the ability to remember the details of little stories the doctor read aloud to deducing how to make various shapes with red and white triangles painted on cubes. The tests revealed I had some deficit in memory and what the medical profession calls the "executive function" of the brain. Dr. Rambeau said that both could be the result of mental illness, but they also could be caused by the psychiatric medications I was taking. She and I agreed I had no choice but to take the drugs, as they were my best shot at staying out of the hospital, so there seemed nothing to do but continue on and hope the cognitive problems did not worsen.

My book on climate change came out in the fall of 2012. By the spring of 2013, I was casting around for a new topic about which to write. I talked with my agent about several different possibilities. After some discussion and considerable thought, I decided to translate the scientific research about mountain-building processes into a document the lay reader might find interesting. One of the advantages of the subject was that my undergraduate advisor at Princeton was a recognized expert in the field. I emailed him, sketched some basic ideas for the book, and asked him if he would cooperate with a writing project that would include portrayals of him and his work studying the mountains of the American West, Alaska, British Columbia, and eventually Bhutan in south Asia. Some of my undergraduate and graduate coursework had been on the topic of mountain building. I bought several scientific books on the process and got to work.

What I read in the books I was studying seemed at least generally familiar. But it had been over 20 years since I had been a student, and I was very rusty when it came to the science in question. I found I had great difficulty with my self-assigned reading. Although the content of the books felt vaguely familiar, I was appalled to find how much I struggled to understand what I had been able to successfully study when I was younger. It wasn't long until the books I had purchased gave me headaches as I tried to glean the gist of the research findings on which they were based.

Again and again, I sat down to carefully read the technical material, but all I seemed able to do was flounder in my attempt to study what I had at one time understood. One of the problems, I decided, was that I would wrestle with a few pages of prose and technical diagrams on, say, Saturday morning, but not be able to really remember what I had learned when I again sat down to study on Sunday afternoon. In the end, I just couldn't make progress because of my cognitive problems. My clouded thinking and memory problems meant that I had to give up the book idea because I simply was no longer sharp enough to pull it off.

I faced similar cognitive problems at work. At times it felt like I was in a fog, perhaps of the sort a person experiences when the effects of a heavy cold are combined with a high dose of antihistamines. I had problems sometimes with basic tasks on my computer, let alone with the complex challenges of editing technical prose outside my training. I drank lots of black coffee and did everything I could to perform as well as possible. I was helped daily by my assistant, Susan, who did everything from reminding me how certain computer functions worked to keeping me aware of all the moving parts embedded in multi-million-dollar grant proposals. My debt to Susan had always been large, but it grew as I wrestled with cognitive issues. In late April of 2014, I had an experience that shocked me about how much my memory seemed to be slipping.

At church, I was part of an ongoing book discussion group; each Sunday we read a chapter of a book and talked about it. One Sunday we met and discussed the last chapter of the book we had been studying from the late winter into the spring. We agreed we wouldn't read a book over the summer, so we'd next take up a new book in late August when the local school year began. But on the following Sunday, I showed up to talk about the old book, thinking we were to discuss the last chapter of it. I simply had no recollection of our finishing the book and agreeing we wouldn't start to read another until the end of the summer. The memory loss was more than spooky. I wracked my brains for any recollection of the previous Sunday but could find none.

When next I saw Dr. Rambeau, I complained more emphatically to her about my intellectual decline. I explained that it was interfering with my day job and had made me give up my proposed book topic in my moonlighting job, namely writing. I also related to her the memory gap I had experienced at Church and explained I was shocked about it. In response to my report of more significant problems, Rambeau sent me for a consultation with a neurologist new to the region.

I was apprehensive about the consultation and asked a friend from church to go with me. I was glad for Dean's company because I didn't know what to expect in terms of diagnosis and prognosis, and I felt intimidated at the thought of seeing a neurologist. The doctor did a brief exam and listened to my tale of cognitive problems including the memory lapse at church. He then launched into a discussion of dementia and what it meant for individuals in his practice.

Since the time my elderly parents began to experience dementia, I had feared that diagnosis in myself more than anything, including terminal illness from cancer, heart failure, or other maladies. As I saw it, I wanted to die with my wits about me, and I would trade years of life for a death I could experience with my full faculties. The diagnosis of dementia changed my expectations of my future, alarming me because it was the one thing I had feared with great intensity and for a long time.

Dean and I discussed what the doctor had said as we drove home from Lewiston where the neurologist practiced. There was no getting around the fact I had been given a death sentence, and the one I had so strongly hoped to avoid. Dean dropped me off at home, and I took my dog on a walk to give me a little time to cogitate on the significance of the doctor's visit. Clearly, as I thought things over, the day would soon come when I couldn't work even at a simple job. Who would take care of me as dementia progressed and I became imbecilic? I was depressed and afraid when I returned home. Usually, exercise helps me process important events, but even a long walk with my faithful dog couldn't help me see how to adapt to the diagnosis I had been given.

As it happened, Dr. Rambeau had also ordered another round of testing with the neuropsychologist I had seen two years previously. That exam came up in a couple of weeks. I wasn't feeling well when I took the test – the stress of the dementia diagnosis had taken a real toll on me, robbing me of sleep.

I was also feeling the undercurrent of depression beginning to tug at me. This time the cognitive testing lasted only half a day, rather than a full one. The doctor said the results were similar to when I had seen him earlier, I showed deficits in memory and executive function, but the deficits were mild as such things go, and were not significantly different from what they had been. This time I also tested like someone who had attention deficit disorder or ADD. That finding seemed at odds with my success in school and in professional-level work, but the test of attention, the doctor said, was consistent with a diagnosis of ADD.

I related to the neuropsychologist the story of my memory loss at church. He listened to that, understanding why it had spooked me, but he said his testing did not indicate I had dementia. I was encouraged but also confused. Clearly, I had some cognitive problems, and from my experience of myself, I could only say they were growing. Were these problems the first phase of dementia, or were they simply the effect of mental illness or the medications I was taking to treat that illness? As I thought over what the two doctors had said to me, one clearly saying I had dementia and one denying it, I was quite confused.

Within days of the second consultation about my cognitive issues, I became more depressed. Soon I was in an emotional tailspin. The rattlesnakes on the floor were more frequently and more clearly present. I didn't know how I could responsibly respond to what the two doctors had told me. Should I tell my supervisor at work that I might have dementia – or then again, I might not? My thinking was confused and went around in small circles over and over again. I called Dr. Rambeau's office and reported I was having sleep problems and a great intensity and circularity in my thinking. Relaying information through the nurse, the doctor adjusted my medication.

The change didn't help. I felt more and more depressed. I called Rambeau's office again and she prescribed a small amount of my old friend Zoloft, a commonly used anti-depressant. The plan was to start small and gradually move to higher doses over time to avoid being crippled by physical side effects – which for me are headache and nausea.

The small amount of Zoloft I had in my bloodstream made no difference to what was happening. I was being sucked down into the vortex of major depression. Each day was worse than the one before, with very dark thoughts about death dominating my mind and robbing me of sleep at night. I was still trying to work, but I had enormous problems concentrating. The day came I called in sick rather than trying to function intellectually. Within hours my depression grew exponentially, threatening to swallow me completely. Soon I wanted to die. When I recognized I had reached that point, and that my life would be in danger when the will to act was united with my fully depressed thinking, I called my minister. We talked about what was happening, and she agreed to give me a ride to the psychiatric ward about an hour from my hometown in Lewiston.

It was greatly discouraging to go back to the locked ward environment. I felt leaden as I walked through the main doors of the hospital. Nothing in me wanted to be institutionalized again. My minister encouraged me with the thought that I had done this before, lived through the dark time, and been restored to something approximating health, with a return to professional work and to my responsibilities at home taking care of my mother. All that was true, I knew, but I felt such hopelessness and despair I could only cry as we waited to be checked in at the emergency room, a process necessary for admission to the psychiatric ward upstairs.

As I was to learn, two significant changes had been made at the hospital since I had been there four years previously. One was that doctors from the clinic where Rambeau practiced no longer saw the patients in the hospital. In the past, a patient had had the same doctor as an in-patient as an out-patient, guaranteeing good continuity of care. For whatever reason, the hospital had changed its policy. In-patients were now seen by doctors who practiced solely within the confines of the locked ward. Only when released from the hospital would patients see the doctor they were used to at the out-patient clinic. Secondly, patients in the ward were no longer visited by a psychologist who ran group meetings in the mornings. In what I assumed was a cost-cutting measure, patients were simply on their own in this respect, although visited one-on-one each day by a psychiatrist or a psychiatric nurse practitioner.

I was assigned an aging psychiatrist I will call Dr. Smith. On the first full day I was in the ward, the psychiatrist spent a lot of time taking a detailed history of me. He delved into my past and asked many questions about my family of origin. I urged him to call Dr. Rambeau for input about what was to be done. He said he would do that, but that to treat me he needed to understand my past and my family life. I answered his questions as best I could. At his prompting I told him about my alcoholic grandfather and uncle, relating how I had grown up in a small university town in a stable family, and then trying to convey to him the illness that had blossomed in me when I was a teenager.

Perhaps because he had spent so much time with me, I had a favorable impression of Dr. Smith after that first session. The next day, however, things didn't seem so positive. He gave me a small sermon about the problems in the profession of psychiatry in recent years. From Smith's perspective, things were bad and getting worse. He explained that the problems hinged on an over-reliance on medication and the failure to examine family history before treatment began. When the sermon was over, the doctor said he would taper me down and off the antipsychotic I was taking. That made sense to me if it was a maneuver meant to make room for a new drug from that family of medications. At my request, the doctor increased my dose of Zoloft, the antidepressant. We agreed to a schedule that would ramp the dose up quickly. I knew that would mean more significant side effects for me to endure, but I would put up with the headache and nausea in the hopes that higher levels of Zoloft might help ease the depression that had engulfed me.

The days went by in the psychiatric ward. I slept little and suffered a lot, swimming in grief. In my better hours, I worked on jigsaw puzzles with my fellow patients and dribbled and shot basketballs in the exercise room when we were granted access to that facility. Each day I met with Dr. Smith. He continued to lecture me on how modern psychiatry was flawed because it didn't pay enough attention to family history and the early dynamics of personal life. His profession, Smith told me, was getting worse and worse. He genuinely seemed to want to convince me of what he said.

I was too ill to argue with him about the importance of medications for helping the seriously ill stay alive and function fully in society. His sermons reminded me of the very first psychiatrist I had dealt with at Harvard, the elderly woman who didn't give me any medications and insisted my problems stemmed from the fact I had been raised in a church-going family. I thought Smith was wrong in what he said about psychiatry, but he was my doctor in a locked ward, and I was merely a patient, so I bit my tongue.

Dr. Smith decreased the antipsychotics I had been on, one step at a time, day after day. At some point, he said he had spoken to Dr. Rambeau on the phone.

"She wants you to take Latuda," he said, referring to an antipsychotic with proven anti-depressant effects. "But Latuda won't help you."

I certainly didn't know how we could be sure of Latuda's effects without trying it. If Latuda was what Dr. Rambeau wanted, that greatly mattered in my book. Why not start the medication my ongoing psychiatrist wanted me to take? I longed to talk to Rambeau directly and tell her what was happening to my medications in the hospital. The antipsychotic I had been taking was now tapered down to nearly nothing and no drug in that family had been started to replace it. That was the same pattern of treatment that had happened in the summer of 2010 and led to two periods of long and miserable hospitalizations in the fall during which I was tremendously ill.

Dr. Smith's treatment of me then took an even more surprising turn. He asked if I had ever tried amphetamines for my illness. I said no, I had not. Would I be interested in a trial of Adderall, the medical name for a drug containing amphetamines? All I knew was that we needed to try something more than increasing Zoloft and eliminating the antipsychotic I was on. I agreed to a trial of Adderall, in part because I knew it was a treatment for attention deficit disorder that the neuropsychologist had seen in his testing data. I explained that to Dr. Smith.

"You don't have ADD," he said to me with finality in his voice. "You track very well in our conversations. Don't believe a doctor who says you have ADD."

I didn't know what to make of what the three doctors had now said to me. Did I have dementia or just cognitive problems related to mental illness? Did I have ADD or was I just an absent-minded intellectual? If I had been well, I could perhaps have researched the issues and come to my own conclusions. But I was far too ill for such work – and I had no access to the internet.

Two days before I was to be discharged Dr. Smith's treatment plan became clearer. "I don't think you are bipolar," he said. "You are simply depressed. You need to examine your family life as a child to find the roots of your illness."

I was startled by this statement from the doctor. Because I was deeply ill, I didn't have the wit to respond to him. I could have said that there was evidence in his hands I wasn't simply depressed. If he had looked at the record of my hospitalizations in 2010, he would have seen I was euphoric for hours amid suicidal depression. If he had asked more questions about my symptoms and fewer about my alcoholic grandfather, he could have learned about the explosions of thought that sometimes occurred in my mind, about the experience of what I termed "dawn screaming hell," about the impossibly brilliant songbirds I had seen on Easter Sunday, and so much more that fit with a bipolar diagnosis and not one of simple depression. I stammered out a phrase or two about all this to Dr. Smith but he wouldn't listen to me. He knew what my problem was and again referred me to the need to examine my family of origin for the cause of the psychiatric issues that had crippled me through the decades.

I thought things over as best I could in my ill state. One thing seemed clear to me: I had entered the hospital because my suicidal thinking was becoming intrusive and, I thought, dangerous. While in the hospital I had developed a specific plan to kill myself, namely by drinking a lot of alcohol and taking all the sedating drugs I had at home. But throughout my stay in the psychiatric ward, Dr. Smith had not asked me any questions about suicidal thoughts or plans. When I was discharged, he shook my hand but didn't go over with me what I should do if suicidal thinking overwhelmed me.

From experience with the ward, I knew a more normal discharge process would include asking who I would call if suicidal thoughts posed a danger to me, and how I could keep myself safe at home. In the hospital and as I was leaving, Dr. Smith never asked about my thoughts and plans for suicide. In at least that respect, my confused mind told me quite clearly that Dr. Smith was a decidedly poor psychiatrist. As I thought it over, I realized at a deep level that once a person enters a locked ward, it's a crapshoot, the kind of treatment one will receive.

I was just as ill when I left the hospital as I had been when I entered it. But I wanted to be discharged so that I could get away from Dr. Smith and return for medical treatment to my own psychiatrist. I thus went home, deeply depressed and with blazing but circular thoughts racing through my tormented brain. I had lost weight and strength due to this round of illness. I knew I was in deep trouble, but all I could do was hang on and accept the encouraging words my friends and family offered me.

Just before I was discharged from the hospital, the social worker in the psychiatric ward had set up an appointment for me to see Dr. Rambeau in the outpatient clinic. A friend from church drove me to that appointment and I returned to the care of a doctor who I hoped could help. Rambeau did not disappoint me. She spent a lot of time listening to what had driven me to seek refuge in the hospital, what had happened in the locked ward, and how difficult life still was for me even on a significant dose of Zoloft. She listened as I told her I didn't think the amphetamines Smith had me on were helpful. They gave me a temporary mood boost shortly after I swallowed the pills, but that wore off within hours and the drug seemed to make sleeping even more unlikely than it had been when I entered the ward.

I explained my thinking was going around in small circles, over and over again. I simply could not command my thoughts but was a victim of them. Rambeau asked me about suicidal thinking and it was a relief to tell her about my plans to kill myself with a combination of alcohol and an overdose of medications.

Rambeau said she wanted to start me on a small dose of Latuda, the antipsychotic known for having anti-depressant effects.

"We'll gradually increase it," she said. "But I also want you to see your psychologist on a regular basis."

I explained that I hadn't seen him for a long time and was no longer an established patient.

"I don't think he has room in his practice for taking me back on," I said. "I've heard he isn't taking new patients."

"May I call him on your behalf?" Rambeau said to me.

I thought about that for just a moment and then gladly accepted. Rambeau then looked at her schedule and made some time to see me the following week. She had to work hard, it was clear, to squeeze me in, but she did so and I was deeply grateful for that fact.

It was early August when I first saw Dr. Rambeau. As the month unfolded, I took more Latuda as per her instructions. Each week, she made time in her schedule to see me and always very carefully asked me how suicidal I was. Good as her word, she called my former psychologist and whatever she said to him worked in my favor. He called me and I started to see him again on a regular basis. With his help, I digested what Dr. Smith had done in the hospital. I considered making a complaint to the hospital administration about Smith. He had ignored the issue that had brought me to the hospital – intrusive suicidal thinking – and he had taken me off the one drug I was taking for bipolar effects.

He had concentrated his treatment of me on discussing my family history and giving me amphetamine – a medication not recognized as a normal treatment for either bipolar disorder or simple depression. In sum, I thought I had good grounds for complaint, but I was still quite ill and I decided against investing my time and energy into such an undertaking.

I started the month of August gravely ill, hardly able to take care of myself, let alone my mother who still lived in my house. As the month progressed, I had a number of ups and downs, but I also gradually became more stable and less suicidal. The Latuda helped lift my depression. I got off the amphetamines and started to sleep a bit more. I walked my dog longer distances and swam some laps, activities that helped me eat and sleep incrementally better. By the end of August, everything was looking up and I returned to work half-time. After Labor Day, I made the commitment to full-time employment. Very quickly I was back in the saddle again and I gave Rambeau the credit because she had given me Latuda, squeezed me into her schedule every week so she could monitor my suicidal thoughts until the medication took hold, and taken the initiative to get me back into my psychologist's practice.

As the late summer dissolved into autumn, my moods were stable, and suicidal thoughts stopped coming to mind. I was as well as I can be. But my cognitive problems cropped up more and more often. I went about my job and, with my assistant's invaluable and daily help, I accomplished some significant things. But both my memory and my concentration were poor.

One day in November I was working on a project and I decided I needed to email my supervisor, the associate dean for research in my part of the university, to ask him a question about what I should do with respect to a faculty member's work. My hands paused at the keyboard as I cast around in my mind for my boss's name. I simply couldn't think of it. I waited for a minute, then tried again, but his name didn't come to mind. I couldn't ask my assistant for my boss's name without seeming a full idiot. I tried again and again to recollect his name but to no avail. Acting on a scrap of inspiration, I went to the web and looked up my part of the university, knowing that an associate dean would be listed as a significant administrator.

Sure enough, I found Jim Moyer on the web. Once I saw the name, it was familiar, but I was alarmed to realize I had been unable, for some minutes, to think of it on my own. Armed with the information I needed, I was able to email my supervisor my question, but I went home that night with a strong sense of how spooky my memory losses were becoming. In late November the same thing happened. I was at work and could not think of the boss's name. I cast around in my head, thinking of other people's names in our office. I had no problem with the name of the assistant dean, the man who had visited me in the psych ward four years previously. But Jim Moyer's name eluded me. Again, I had to look his name up on the web. In December, the whole process was repeated. The only good thing was that I finally had the sense to write Jim's name on a Post-it note and stick it to the wall above my computer. That solved the specific problem, but it didn't in any way address the broader issue of what was wrong. For some reason, the part of my brain that should store my supervisor's name wasn't working, and I wasn't even successfully relearning it by looking it up time and time again.

Memory wasn't my only problem. My ability to concentrate and think clearly at work was clearly compromised. I did everything I could to help myself, going to bed early, drinking black coffee all morning long, and giving myself pep talks about focusing as best I could. But I wasn't able to do my job well and I knew it. Young faculty, in particular, relied on me for guidance and advice, and I was frustrated to find I couldn't think well enough to respond to them as someone in my job should. In early December, I got a letter that shocked and pained me. It was from the hospital outpatient clinic where Dr. Rambeau practiced. The letter simply said that Rambeau was "no longer seeing patients" at the clinic. No explanation was given for this complete change of affairs.

The letter reached me on a Saturday, just before I was to go on a six-mile walk with my friend Becky. As we ambled along with our dogs, I told Becky the news. It felt like I had experienced a physical blow to my guts, so great was my sense of loss. Becky listened sympathetically to my tale of woe, and that simple fact helped me with the first stage of adjustment to the news. On Monday I called the clinic and spoke to a staff member. She said people were surprised by the announcement of Rambeau's departure, but that the staff didn't know anything more than that Rambeau was gone. I was offered an appointment with another psychiatrist and I accepted it, but I still struggled to think that the doctor who had, from my perspective, saved my life in August was suddenly gone. What had happened, I wondered? I talked to my psychologist about the matter and he called his contacts in the area but couldn't get any more information than I had been given. Rambeau was gone, and that was that.

Christmas was a good but stressful time. The upside of the holidays was several days spent with family and friends. The stressful part was born of my realization that I was having repeated and serious cognitive problems and that things were worsening. I talked to my psychologist about my inability to remember the boss's name. I explained to him that without the help of my assistant, I wasn't able to do my own part of the work in my office. All too often, I was in a dense fog and couldn't think clearly. In sum, I was no longer able to do my job responsibly, and I wanted to squarely recognize that even though being honest about my abilities scared me out of my wits. I also talked to my brother and sister-in-law about my cognitive decline and what it meant for me at work. My sister-in-law, Krista, was at that time a counselor in the local disability action office, so she was familiar with how various people have problems performing in different ways on the job.

Sitting around the dining room table, we brainstormed about how I might be able to work as long as I was able. I appreciated the support of my relatives more than I could express, but the bottom line remained I was having major, even massive, problems doing my job.

A return to daily working life arrived soon after the Christmas and New Year's holidays. One afternoon, mired in intellectual mud and unable to think clearly, I called my sister-in-law. I asked for an appointment to come see her at her office and formally ask for her professional help. On the appointed day, a church friend and I went to the disability office in a nearby town, Moscow, Idaho, which is some ten miles away from Pullman. We discussed my problems remembering even such things as the boss's name. Krista told me I needed to talk honestly with the human resources department of my university, explaining to them the challenges I faced. I knew she was right although I also suspected doing so would set in motion a chain of events very likely to be truly significant to my career. Still, I called my university's human resources department and got an appointment to see a staffer.

Krista came with me the day I was to go to human resources. In a small, windowless office, we talked to a young staff member about my problems. She was clearly sobered by my tale, especially when I got to the part about time and time again forgetting the boss's name.

"You can't even work as a greeter at Walmart if you can't remember the boss's name!" she interjected. In response to a question from the staffer, I said I was 54 years old, and going to turn 55 in just a couple of weeks.

"That's good," she said. "At age 55 you'll be eligible for disability retirement. That will give you the benefit of being able to buy health insurance through the state."

I accepted some forms to fill out. Krista and I made an appointment to meet with the young staffer's supervisor for an introduction to the nitty-gritty details of what disability retirement would mean. I was told not to discuss what was in the works with anyone in my office, not my assistant and not my supervisor.

My stress levels reached high as I tried to take in all the human resource staffer had told me. I longed to discuss it all with my colleagues, and I didn't understand why I shouldn't, but since I needed the help of the human resources department, I decided I had to do what I was told and not discuss my situation with anyone at work. Krista and I returned another day and I was deeply glad she was with me because I couldn't really take in all that was discussed with the higher-level staffer. On the good side, I was eligible to apply for private disability insurance through a policy I had as an employee of the university. The benefits were good but would run for only a year and three quarters. Social Security benefits were much lower, but if granted, they could run until I was 65. I could access my modest retirement account at some point and help pay my bills, at least for a time. Nothing about any of these matters was certain, and we didn't know if the private insurance company, nor the Social Security Administration would grant me benefits but there were at least some things I could apply for.

My birthday approached rapidly. I consulted with my sister-in-law and decided my last day at work would be the Friday after I turned 55. It pained me not to discuss this with my supervisor and my assistant if only to give them notice I was going to leave my job. But I did as the human resource staffers had asked and remained silent. On that Friday, safely arrived at age 55, I asked my supervisor's secretary if I could see him. She gave me an appointment near the end of the work day. I then talked to my assistant, telling her all I knew of my medical situation, the cognitive problems I was having, and my decision that the most responsible course of action I could take was to elect disability retirement. She wished me well as I tried to deal with my medical problems and navigate the next phase of life. We vowed to keep in touch with each other. Soon it was time to talk to my boss, explain that I was immediately leaving my job, and give him the name of someone I thought could do my work very well if he cared to hire her. For his part, Jim expressed dismay that I was leaving,

"I'm not arguing with the diagnosis," he said. "But everyone thinks your office is doing excellent work."

I indicated I was glad to hear that assessment, but I knew my cognitive problems and wanted to leave my job before people said I was dropping the ball.

As five o'clock arrived, I put my personal belongings into a couple of boxes and carried them to my car. In the dark and cold of a February evening, I began to face what my life would be like having started declaring to the world that I was disabled, quite unable to do my job. I felt that my role in the world changed abruptly as I drove home, leaving my employment behind.

The stress I felt was incredible. My whole identity was somehow suddenly unclear and my body responded to my walking away from work with flood-levels of adrenalin. I tried to eat but lost five pounds in two weeks, bringing my weight to 128 pounds. I tried to sleep at night, but mental rattlesnakes sometimes swarmed over the floor around my bed. But on the good side, I didn't go into a full emotional tailspin as I had when one doctor had told me I had dementia while another said I didn't. The antipsychotic drug called Latuda was working; it held my mind together even while my aging brain was feeling a great deal of stress.

Slowly, and not without some stumbling, I made it from late winter to early spring. I started volunteering at the local humane society as a dog walker, which united my love of all things canine with my need to exercise daily. Additionally, I began volunteering at a local food bank each Saturday morning when groceries were distributed to folks in need of assistance. Both volunteer jobs guaranteed I was physically active and involved in the community, positive developments that helped me both because I enjoyed the work and because it seemed valuable. In the spring, I was granted disability benefits by the private insurance company that cooperated with my employer. Although the benefits were slated to run for only 21 months, they significantly boosted my spirits. It was easier, I found, to do my volunteer work as well as sleep at night now that I had the assurance of income for at least the immediate future.

Other good news soon reached me. A regional newspaper ran an advertisement welcoming Dr. Jaime Rambeau to a large medical practice in Lewiston, the same city where she had been working in the hospital clinic. I was happy my favorite psychiatrist had resurfaced, and I called to set up an appointment. My friend Becky, whom I often walk with on Saturdays, kindly came with me when I went to see Rambeau and establish my record with her new office. As usual, the good doctor didn't disappoint. From memory, she knew what medications I was taking and which I had previously tried under her direction. She typed all that data into the computer system as we talked our way through my history. I was considerably reassured about my psychiatric care as Becky and I drove through the countryside to return home.

More challenges, however, were also in store for me. On the last Friday of May, my mother was taken ill. She had pain in her abdomen that narcotics could not control. By noon the two of us were in the emergency room. Late afternoon, my brother, my minister, and I were consulting with the ER doctor about what was happening. My 89-year-old mother, who had a list of major medical problems as long as my arm, was experiencing something none of us would have predicted – she had appendicitis. My mother, who by that time had intravenous morphine dripping into her body, was too drugged to meaningfully talk with the doctor in charge of the ER. It fell to my brother and me to ask him what her situation really entailed. He explained that a surgeon could operate on her, but she was very frail and had significant breathing problems. Those factors meant her recovery from surgery would likely be complicated at best. Alternatively, the ER doctor could fill her with antibiotics, transfer her to a hospital room, and hope her body might fight the infection.

"We're now treating children who have appendicitis with antibiotics rather than surgery," he said, "but that doesn't necessarily mean it's a good option for your mother. What you need to understand is that there are only bad choices in front of you. Doing surgery may lead to your mother's death, and not doing surgery may also do so."

My brother and I discussed the situation with my minister listening in. The doctor said he couldn't give us any odds about outcomes from the choice before us, just saying the risk of death was very real whichever route we traveled. Since there didn't seem to be clear reasons to choose surgery, Nils and I opted not to put our elderly mother through all that an appendectomy would entail.

Soon my mother was moved to a regular hospital room. After a couple more hours, she seemed to be stable, so my brother and I went to our respective homes for the night. We made a plan that I would come to be with my mother first thing in the morning, and my brother or sister-in-law would come later in the day, the three of us spelling each other. When I got home that night I was deeply stressed, but I just barely had the wit to call my mother's best friend, a woman she had known from church for more than 40 years. I explained my mother's situation to Mary, saying I just wanted her to know what was happening. In the morning I found my mother much improved. The antibiotic had clearly helped overnight. Her pain was down, and her narcotics were much more limited. After greeting me, she sat up and took some nourishment. I was relieved and cautiously optimistic about her prospects. We talked with each other, dealt with nurses and other staff members who came into the room and spoke warmly with Mary, my mother's good friend, when she arrived with her husband for a visit.

In the afternoon my sister-in-law came to take over. I said goodbye to my mother, who seemed in pretty good shape. But as Krista later told me, everything changed in the early evening. Pain spread across my mother's abdomen. My sister-in-law was with her when the doctor told my mother she was dying. My mother took in that news as best she could. She was given a large dose of morphine to help with the pain. As she sank rapidly, she talked a bit with Krista. When her words were clearly each costing her, she said simply, "I can see the dark, but I'm moving toward the light." She was unconscious when my brother arrived. He later said that she simply breathed more and more slowly, then stopped breathing altogether.

I got the word of my mother's death in the morning. I thought again and again about the decision my brother and I had made to opt for antibiotics but no surgery. I wondered if we had done the right thing. But I was sure my mother would not have wanted to end up in intensive care, an outcome we thought was pretty likely if she had surgery and developed complications, especially with her breathing problems. As it happened, she was seven weeks shy of turning 90, and although I knew she had wanted to make it to that birthday, I also thought Nils and I had done the best we could to make a difficult choice given what the doctor in the emergency room had explained to us. And I called to mind the words of an old doctor in the hospital hallway who had said to me he was fully comfortable with the decision my brother and I had made.

Nils and I met with Henry, a staffer from the local funeral home. My mother wished to be cremated as my father had been before her. Henry asked if either of us wanted to be present when our mother's remains were rolled into the crematory furnace. I said yes, I did. A time was set and my minister and a friend from church met me at the funeral home. The two women had known my mother and were present that morning to support me during my loss. My minister read the prayer of committal, including the "ashes to ashes" phrase, and Henry opened the furnace door and rolled the box containing my mother's remains into the furnace. He then asked me if I wanted to throw the switch to start the final fire. I didn't hesitate because I wanted to do everything I could for my mother, and I did as Henry indicated I could. Once I threw the switch, a roar from multiple natural gas flames filled the crematory. After a minute, we departed.

I found the grieving process I went through for my mother to be quite different than that for my father. Waves of memories didn't wash over me as had earlier been the case. I missed my mother, but I didn't want her back in the condition she had left us, frail and with a host of medical problems. I was surprised that I cried very little. I wept just before going to the crematory. I was in the kitchen when I started to sob. I sat down on the floor and Buster Brown, my faithful dog, came to me and licked me in the face.

That helped ease my pain and I was dry-eyed the remainder of the day.

My brother choked up at our mother's memorial service, but I didn't cry. Was my reaction partly dictated by the psychiatric medications I was taking, or did the years of caring for my mother in my home give me time to grieve before her death? I couldn't say, but I talked in detail with my psychologist about what I felt about my mother's passing. Grief, perhaps, is different each time one encounters it, regardless of psychiatric medications.

It always takes emotional energy to absorb the death of a family member, a process that stretches on for months or years. But as I was grieving, I was helped in daily life by the excellent housemate I had acquired. Mary is a friend of mutual friends, someone I had found by word of mouth as I looked for a housemate to help cover the monthly bills. She is a dedicated Lutheran who, among several other jobs at her church, is in charge of part of a network of congregations that works to help house the homeless in our community.

She is a positive person and a talkative one who shares what she is reading and thinking. She works as a field and greenhouse technician at the local land-grant university where I worked. Mary's most important characteristic to me is that she dares to live with someone with a major mental illness. For that, I am deeply grateful. And as frosting on the cake, Mary brought a Corgi to my household who gets along well with my dog. So, we are a two-person, two-canine household, complete with a fenced backyard big enough for fetching Frisbees and a dog door that allows the pooches access to the outside.

As the calendar pages turned deeper into the summer of 2015, I came to realize that in one respect the death of my parents freed me. I had tried not to worry them for decades, even though I was gravely ill. Although I time and time again asked for their help, at the same time I didn't want to distress them. With both of them gone, I felt freer to explore and understand the depth of my illness.

One day in July of 2015 I came home from my regular monthly visit with Dr. Rambeau, the psychiatrist. That evening I had the experience of hearing an encoded message imbedded in the sound of my printer processing a job. As is most commonly the case for me, I couldn't understand the communication that was being pounded into my brain by the sound, but that didn't lessen the importance of the message. As always, the auditory hallucination ripped my attention away from what I was doing and plunged me into a maddening experience. When it was over, I reflected on what had happened. Acting on impulse as much as clear thinking, I took a piece of paper and wrote a memo to my psychiatrist and my psychologist by hand. I briefly explained that I had heard things like maniacal laughter and encoded messages since middle school. Only once had I heard what I termed the voice of God, but the experience of encoded messages was common. Although I had denied to doctors that I had auditory hallucinations in my adult life, I wanted to come clean and let two doctors I trusted know what had been the case for so very long. I made copies of the memo and put them into the mail to both my doctors.

As it happened, I saw the psychologist first. We went over the brief but significant note I had sent him. I explained why I had for so long denied my auditory experiences. The pediatrician I had seen in childhood had seemed to warn me that discussing such things would be a horrible idea. Then, as an adult, I learned enough about psychiatric states to know that auditory hallucinations were a significant symptom that would likely mean I wasn't merely depressed but had even more serious problems. I simply hadn't been able to tell the doctors what I sometimes heard. I knew I was ill, but I feared a diagnosis of even more serious problems. Finally, I didn't want to worry my friends and family, especially my parents.

I told the psychologist I was sorry I hadn't been forthcoming sooner. He wasn't miffed that I hadn't given him the full picture of illness. Indeed, he warmly thanked me for the letter. We then discussed in detail what my auditory hallucinations are like. He got out his diagnostic handbook and together we went over the key features of bipolar disorder and the spectrum of schizophrenia. After studying the criteria together, it seemed clear the best diagnosis for my life-long condition was schizoaffective disorder.

I knew enough to be sure the new diagnosis would mean a worse prognosis than I had previously had, one with increasing cognitive problems and illness my constant companion until death. In that sense, admitting to auditory events of the sort that have dogged me was more than sobering. But it was also a relief to speak clearly about my problems and how challenged I am sometimes to function normally.

The following week I saw my psychiatrist for my regular monthly appointment. We discussed my letter and the auditory hallucinations that have been an ongoing issue. The psychiatrist agreed that "schizoaffective disorder, bipolar subtype" was my best diagnosis. I told the psychiatrist I had now told her everything – I had no more troubles to confess. The briefest of smiles flashed across her face. Again, I felt relief to have told a doctor all of my problems. As I drove home from that appointment through the countryside, I was simply grateful I had lived long enough to reach a point where I could tell the doctors everything.

My new diagnosis did not change my treatment. I was already taking two antipsychotics, so there was nothing to add in that department. Like patients with bipolar disorder, people who are schizoaffective are advised to take psychiatric medications each day and, if possible, see a psychologist or counselor for help navigating life. I was already doing all that, and was living without alcohol, and with daily physical exercise. So, the new diagnosis didn't change anything except my understanding of how ill I had always been. Soon I was explaining my life-long auditory symptoms and the new diagnosis to family and friends. Although some people may have been surprised at the extent of illness I have always lived with, everyone I talked with was supportive. Next, it was time to read up in the medical literature about schizoaffective disorder. I was surprised to find that compared to schizophrenia and bipolar disorder, there were almost no technical articles about schizoaffective disorder. I wondered if I was somehow doing my computer searches incorrectly. By chance, I had found the name and email address of the scientist in charge of research into "schizophrenia spectrum" illnesses at the National Institutes of Health. I wrote to the woman in question who kindly took the time to answer me. She said there really were almost no technical pieces about my disorder. She attached to her email a few articles that did address my new diagnosis. I read them with care but they added very little to what I had already surmised from the doctors.

The bottom line was that the prognosis I now faced was one step worse than it had been with bipolar disorder, but not as bad as full schizophrenia would have been. Unsurprisingly, I was having cognitive problems – that was to be expected with any diagnosis in the schizophrenic spectrum. I could be glad, in fact, that I am still functioning as much as I am. Although I often am in an intellectual fog, I have been able to finish this book, albeit working from an extensive draft I had written in 2011 when I was still employed. My writing has partly been motivated by the hope this document might be useful to people suffering from schizophrenic spectrum disorders or to their loved ones. If doctors read this book, it may help them in their practice of medicine. Most people on the schizophrenic spectrum simply don't have the skills and abilities to write about their inner experiences, as I have tried to do here.

Finishing this volume's manuscript has given me something to do in retirement and has let me work with what cognitive skills I still have. That, at the end of the day, has been a real help to me as I adjust to a full diagnosis of my considerable problems.

It was in July of 2015 that I wrote to my doctors about the auditory hallucinations that had been with me for so long. In August I began to research what was entailed in applying for Social Security disability benefits. I knew that two out of three first-time applicants are rejected, a sobering proportion, and I had heard that people who have mental illness had a particularly hard time proving to the Social Security Administration they were really ill, and thus unable to work. The application process has its complexities, as shown by the fact that a whole industry has developed to help people navigate the system. Lawyers who specialize in Social Security disability claims are to be found in every phone book. I talked to a paralegal in the city of Spokane and went through an interview process with him.

The bottom line was that, if successful, the lawyer would charge me money out of the benefits I received. My sister-in-law had established an online account for me with Social Security and showed me I could receive about $1600 per month if benefits were granted. That decidedly modest sum wasn't something I wanted to share with a lawyer, and Krista urged me to apply on my own.

I tried to look at the government website for applying online, but the medical information needed coupled with the computer work itself seemed mightily formidable to my foggy brain. But using my research skills honed over the years, I went to the library and found a recent volume I could get through an inter-library loan that addressed how to apply for social security disability. When the 400-page book came, it seemed more than a bit overwhelming. I set the book aside, quite discouraged with my situation. How can someone with cognitive problems master all that's needed to apply for the benefits she might be entitled to?

The next day inspiration hit me. What I needed was an able person who had the time to help me with the application process from soup-to-nuts. I needed someone sharp enough to decide what the relevant sections of the book were, read them, and guide me through the online application. Obviously, the person needed to have a good heart to be willing to help me with the project without remuneration. Rather boldly, I contacted the wife of my colleague Mike, he who had once visited me in the locked psychiatric ward.

Linda is, I knew, an exceedingly sharp person who had recently retired. I explained what I had in mind and asked if she would be so kind as to help me. To my delight, she said she could at least read through the book I had, and see how involved the project looked. I immediately walked over to her house with the book. The very next day she phoned to say the project looked manageable.

Over several days, Linda and I sat at her dining room table in the afternoons and wrestled with what the Social Security Administration seemed to want from me. I would walk home from her house armed with a to-do list of information I was to gather before our next meeting. Nothing was too difficult, but phone calls and web work were required to locate not just contact information for doctors, but such arcana as patient identification numbers in each doctor's office. A short essay was also required, one that addressed why I could no longer work. I drafted a piece that my sister-in-law edited, and Linda inserted it into the relevant box online. Linda and I worked on the project for a week or ten days, saving our labor on the Social Security website at the end of each session. And at the end of that period, we made a good effort toward reaching our goal, but the application needed one more going-over.

As it happened, it was on a Monday in late August, that I met with Dr. Rambeau to discuss my auditory hallucinations. She agreed at that session to change my diagnosis from "Bipolar I, with psychotic features," to "schizoaffective disorder, bipolar subtype." On Tuesday morning I left town with a friend, headed for a two-day trip to the mountains of northwest Washington. On Tuesday afternoon, still in the car, I got a call on my cellphone from the local Social Security office. A woman explained she was calling about my application for disability benefits.

"But I haven't yet applied," I said, "we have not hit the submit button in the online system."

The woman said that I had applied. I protested again that Linda and I had not applied, we were still in the process of working on it.

"And that really matters," I said, "because the psychiatrist changed my diagnosis yesterday. I need to rewrite everything to reflect that fact. I'm telling you, I haven't applied!"

The woman again said that I had applied and that she could see my application on her screen.

"You can't un-apply," she said emphatically. "But you can still change the application for the remainder of the day."

At first, I didn't see how having the rest of the day would change much. My mind raced ahead, wondering if a person could apply for Social Security disability, be rejected, and then appeal on the grounds of a changed diagnosis. I knew that a schizoaffective diagnosis was more serious than a bipolar one. Perhaps with the help of a lawyer, I could make the case that the new diagnosis should be considered on appeal. But appealing hardly seemed a good option as I knew the process in eastern Washington takes two years.

Then a better thought formed in my distressed brain. I called my sister-in-law, reached her on the first try, and explained the situation including the fact I was in a car that was hours from anywhere. Could she go into the website that very afternoon, I asked, and rewrite the application to reflect the fact I now had a schizoaffective diagnosis rather than a bipolar one?

Krista agreed to help. Fortunately, she found the time to sit down with her computer that same afternoon and extensively edit the application. As she worked, I called Linda just to tell her what was happening. Linda was emphatic that nothing we had done should have submitted the application to Social Security. I agreed with her.

From my perspective, Social Security's online application system was flawed, making a significant mistake in somehow bumping my application from a "saved" status to an "applied" one. But when I calmed down, I wondered why the woman with Social Security had called me. She hadn't asked for any information, she had just informed me that I had applied. Perhaps another error was working to my benefit?

I still am confused by the events of that memorable day, but with Krista's help the finalized application stated I had been diagnosed with schizoaffective disorder. Once I returned home and read through Krista's work, I was reassured that the application reflected what Dr. Rambeau's records would show. But the events of that Tuesday didn't give me confidence in Social Security's ability to deal with the systems we citizens must use to relate to the government agency.

After a couple of weeks, I largely set aside my thoughts about everything related to Social Security. I knew the review process could take up to 120 days, a span that reached from late August until Christmas, so I expected to hear about my application in December. But one Saturday in early October I returned from the food bank where I volunteered to find a letter for me from the Social Security Administration. My pulse quickened as I opened the envelope, but I fully expected it would contain only another form for me to fill out or something similar. To my surprise, the form letter stated I was entitled to disability benefits retroactive to August. I read the letter carefully twice through, then set it down on the dining room table. Still disbelieving, I picked it up again and read it for a third time.

Carrying the letter, I quickly walked over to Linda's house and rang the doorbell. She answered and I gave her the news. It seemed so unlikely to me that I had been approved so quickly that I thrust the letter at Linda for her to read. She was, of course, delighted. I called my sister-in-law and shared the glad tidings when I got home. It had taken three of us working together to get the application in, but the effort had been worthwhile. Social Security disability benefits are not generous, but at least I will have something coming in each month and receive the benefit of Medicare. For that, I am deeply grateful and indebted to two able and good women for my benefits.

CHAPTER 9:

REFLECTIONS

In each generation, some young people are singled out to be swept into the major mental illness vortex. They spin downward and find themselves confronting myriad challenges that are part of such things as schizophrenia or bipolar disorder. Their maladies are largely simply problems in brain chemistry, the imbalance of certain neuro-transmitters. But substantial stigma still clings to all sorts of mental illness, making seeking professional help too often unlikely. Even if a young person does talk to a psychologist or counselor, there's no telling how the professional may frame what's happening. He may blame the symptoms on such things as a church upbringing or supposedly bad parenting when, in fact, religious life and devoted parents have been a fine foundation for the patient, not the cause of the disease. Sometimes young people with mental illness experiment with drugs or alcohol to temporarily quiet the demons that haunt them. That can become a whole problem in itself. If young people are truly lucky, they may get effective help from prescription drugs chosen by a psychiatrist.

Medication can indeed help. For the past 7 years, I have had what I consider to be very good luck taking a cocktail of drugs made of two atypical antipsychotics, lithium, and an anti-depressant. I have been stable despite stressors like my mother's death, adapting to a housemate and her dog, and moving with that housemate to a retirement community. I give the medications credit for the fact I've not been hospitalized, and indeed I've not even considered going to the psych ward. It took years to find the combination of drugs that make this stability possible, but with the help of an excellent psychiatrist who focused on symptoms, we found the recipe for helping my peculiar brain to run more evenly. I thank God for the doctor and the meds.

As I look over the landscape of my life's history, I see I had both good and bad luck. Several events were highly unfortunate. As a child, I explained to my pediatrician that I was hearing maniacal laughter ringing in my head. The doctor completely dropped the ball, threatening me in a stern tone with an unknown-to-me professional called a psychiatrist. That conversation shut me down in a way that lasted for years. Following in those footsteps, the doctors at Princeton failed to refer me for psychological or psychiatric help, telling me to drink warm milk and herb tea (literally!).

When I was 19 years old, a psychologist at home diagnosed me as suffering from simple depression, a diagnosis that was right as far as it went but that followed me for far too long. When I finally saw a psychiatrist at Harvard, she said I was depressed and that condition stemmed from the fact I had been raised in church. That was as unhelpful as it could be. A second psychiatrist saw me through my day-to-day suffering, a fact that may have saved my life, but he missed the boat when I asked him if "unexplained joy," as I termed it, was a psychiatric symptom. He simply said it wasn't when he could have said, "Tell me more." If he had heard more about what I meant by "joy," what he would have termed "euphoria," he would most likely have been led to give me a diagnosis of bipolar disorder. That might not have led to useful treatment at the time, simply because psychiatric drugs were still in their infancy, but it might have been useful in other ways. Even at age 54, my bad luck with most doctors continued when a hospital psychiatrist diagnosed me with simple depression. He took me off all antipsychotics, offering me amphetamines for depression. To make matters worse, he wanted to blame my family for my problems, saying I would not be well until I dredged up supposedly negative facts about my childhood.

On the other hand, I had wonderfully good luck in other realms. I made lifelong friends Back East in college, graduate school, and at Quaker Meeting. After I returned home, my good fortune in making friends continued. My comrades helped keep me alive when times were hard and the rattlesnakes were at their most dangerous. And I had wonderfully good luck in my family.

Just as one example of that fact, my parents fed and housed me for years after I left Harvard. Our nightly habit of reading aloud to each other started me down a road that included writing my first book.

Ultimately my diagnosis was changed by a psychiatrist from depression to bipolar disorder. Eventually that led to finding some of the atypical antipsychotic drugs that have been helpful, even though they also have given me Parkinsonism, according to a diagnosis made by a neurologist as I finished this book. When I belatedly told the doctors about my auditory hallucinations, I received what I view as my final diagnosis: my life has been lived on the schizophrenic spectrum, with "schizoaffective disorder, bipolar subtype." My experience of the illness has mostly been high-energy hellishness, what could be termed dysphoric mania or hypomania, such as when I was camping in Nevada and literally didn't sleep at all some nights. Ditto for the nights at Princeton and Harvard and back home, where my thoughts raced all night and I got hardly any sleep.

I've also had significant physical symptoms that took time to diagnose. Since I was a teenager, I've had pain in places in my muscles and around some joints. It took years of mentioning this pain to primary care physicians to finally get a referral to a rheumatologist. That specialist diagnosed me with a malady called fibromyalgia. Happily, as the years have slipped by, that pain has decreased. Perhaps that's because something in my body improved on its own, or perhaps that's because I take prescription anti-inflammatory pills and wear narcotic transdermal patches for pain caused by scoliosis in my back. Either way, the change is welcome because fibromyalgia can be debilitating.

Another issue is less clear. I may sometimes have some smattering of attention deficit disorder (ADD). The neuropsychologist near my hometown diagnosed me with ADD, which fit with my inability to follow along with Lincoln Hollister's lectures in the fall of my senior year at Princeton. Those were the lectures where I ended up with no notes because my mind went off in day-dreams for the whole hour, even though I very much valued the content of what Lincoln was guiding us through. When I was a student (and later in church and faculty meetings), I could day-dream with the best of them even though it was involuntary. I think I don't have major problems with ADD, but maybe it's a small part of the picture of how my brain functions (or doesn't).

But let us get back to the psychiatric angle of what I've experienced during my 63 years. While psychiatric illness has limited my life, it has at times enriched it. The most beautiful experiences I have known have occurred while I was deeply ill. While no one would want to end up in a locked psychiatric ward, I have been blessed to know some of my fellow patients there, as well as the nuns who visit the ward in the Catholic hospital where I have sought refuge. Over the years I've come to deeply respect my fellow patients whose lives are interrupted by episodic accelerations into manic energy, drops into depression, or journeys through the waking nightmare of psychosis due to schizophrenia. Building as much of a life as possible in the context of abrupt catastrophes affecting thought, mood, and judgment takes skill and courage. In particular, I've seen the true heroism evidenced by people from limited backgrounds who successfully put together decent lives against the backdrop of illness and the widespread poverty among people with major mental disorders. Thus, when I'm hospitalized, I try to concentrate on the valuable lessons I can learn from my fellow patients.

Some of my friends on the outside of psych wards have told me they don't understand how I can think there is anything worthwhile in the intervals I've spent as an in-patient. They urge me not to think about what I've experienced in locked wards. To them, angelic beings filling bleachers beyond solid walls are simply nonsensical experiences, like a night filled with vivid dreams after eating too much spicy food. Ditto with the nightmarish and thick darkness that can fill my room at dawn, making me long for the release of death. The best thing to do with my memories of both suffering and euphoria in hospitals is to forget about them, or so I've been told by the well-meaning.

I can't agree with those friends who urge me to forget some of my more extreme experiences. Some of what I've come to know when ill is hope, holding out the promise of full communion with others. And although it's impossible to be glad for medical problems, being mentally ill has been such a large part of my life that I can't imagine my existence without it. Besides that, I hope, I've learned from my condition, including the parts of my life that descents have shaped into strong illness.

Naturally, sometimes I'd be glad to be rid of the mental rattlesnakes, the encoded messages I hear, and the occasional visual or tactile hallucination. But the same tormented brain that produces these experiences surprises me at times with crystal-clear and useful ideas, helping me turn on a dime and make major decisions. I know those whom I call "the normal people" find it odd to think that someone can be harassed by imaginary rattlesnakes all day long, and then find herself launching into what ultimately becomes a successful book project that same evening. But I sometimes think I can recognize good ideas that surge through my brain on waves of hypomanic energy. So, I simply try to do my best to ignore the rattlers and plans for suicide, on the one hand, while making full use of sudden insights that seem promising.

I sometimes wonder how my mystical and psychotic experiences really differ. That's something I have pondered for years. The two types of experiences seem to me to be quite distinct. I would always be glad to have more mystical experiences, like seeing the divine in inanimate objects and feeling one with the world and all the people around me. And those experiences, coupled with life in various Christian congregations, helped propel me to do things like work in a soup kitchen in Cambridge or labor to help house homeless families in the rural Northwest.

Who can object to having such experiences or pursuing such work? One thing is certain: the psychiatrist whom I most valued, Dr. Rambeau, told me the angelic beings I experienced in the basketball room of the hospital were "elements" of my psychosis. But in my mind, since they were linked not to suffering but to a wonderful outpouring of love, the beings who lived behind the sheetrock were a clear example of mystical communion with the divine. And, Lord knows, I needed that uplifting experience when I was living through such a dark and dangerous time. So, while I understand the medical view, in my own mind I cannot say that the chorus of angels was the result of disease.

But without my most common delusion, namely the rattlesnakes on the floor, would I still be the same person I am? That's where major mental illness differs from some physical maladies. I've got a malformed aortic heart valve, quite a lousy feature to have in a pump that's vital to keeping me conscious from one moment to the next. But if the doctors replace my defective valve tomorrow, I don't think it would change me meaningfully. If, on the other hand, they could fix my mental disease and end the rattlesnakes (and perhaps the mystical experiences?), something significant about myself would be radically different. I'm not sure who I'd be.

Obviously, my time since middle school has been shaped by illness. I have dropped into life-threatening episodes of depression more times than I can count. I've also been in dysphoric manic states, both in hospitals and outside institutions. I know a thing or two about psychiatric suffering, as my life with the rattlesnakes makes clear. My problems have limited my life, most particularly in that I didn't make a family of my own. That was and is an enormous loss.

Now, in old age, I spend a lot of time managing mental illness. I'm doing much better at this task than I did when I was young. The largest change is that I don't drink at all. It's clear to me that living sober confers nothing but advantages compared to frequent drinking. While that's true for everyone, it goes double for the mentally ill. Another management issue is that despite having bad knees and progressive scoliosis of the spine, I exercise virtually every day. That takes time, and finding the energy for swimming or serious walking can be difficult. But the exercise is worthwhile because although it doesn't cure me of anything, it does help me get through some energy or anxiety surges, and I like to think it's marginally useful in helping me sleep at night. It also addresses some of the more psychological issues of my condition by volunteering at a food bank and being active in church life. Involvement in community life is useful for everyone, and perhaps in particular for the mentally ill: we need to see ourselves as valuable despite the stigma that still cloaks our condition.

But despite my serious efforts at controlling my mind's behavior by avoiding alcohol, being diligent with exercise, and being involved in community life, it's also true that I always take my cocktail of psychiatric medications in the evening. The drugs are designed to help slow me down, give me some sleep, and change the ratios of certain neurotransmitters in my diseased brain. Unfortunately, even a trio of strong drugs taken each night doesn't rid me of the rattlesnakes that can sometimes still surround my bed as I toss and turn.

Nor do medications specifically designed to combat psychosis free me fully of auditory and other hallucinations. Simply put, I am deeply ill even with the help of a good psychiatrist, a skilled psychologist, and several medications taken daily. But I've been stable for the past 8 years and the drugs are the reason for that accomplishment.

My life is a house built upon the sand, not the solid rock. Maybe I'll kill myself when the rattlers next swarm up onto the bed, truly maddening me with the incredible fear and pain they inflict. It would be understandable if I at some point make that choice, and I do have a plan for it. But I also very much don't want the snakes to win what has now been our 40-year-long struggle with each other. In sum, I am holding my own with the aid of my friends and family, two good mental health practitioners, and several psychiatric medications. That's a victory I try to celebrate a little each day. But as long as I yet live, I know that hospital experiences will likely be woven into the warp and weft of my life because the cocktail of medications can lose their power at any time. I've turned a corner in self-understanding, and I'm able to embrace the simple fact that the hospital is never too far away.

Once, when I was inside the psych ward, and because such a place makes intense conversation a staple of daily life, I closely questioned a visiting Catholic Sister on the nature of prayer. On a good day, when I'm sane and truly at my best, I pursue contemplative prayer, a demanding form of communion with the divine based on silence. But when I'm strongly ill, I cannot discipline my mind to find anything deeper than my moment-by-moment torment. I explained to the Sister my predicament, being too ill to pray as a contemplative would and too proud as an intellectual to find meaning in the traditional words of spoken prayer. I asked the Sister, could I pray – or was it just impossible?

Nothing about prayer is impossible, she assured me. And, she said with the quiet strength and grace I've come to associate with nuns in psych wards, our lives themselves are our most real prayers.

"Even when we are engulfed by pain?" I asked.

"Especially then," she answered.

In my deeply depressed state at the time, I took comfort in the idea that if I did kill myself – an option very much on the table – my final act in this world would be a prayerful one by the nun's standard because it surely would be informed by searing pain. Now that I've recovered from that round of suicidal thinking, and my mind doesn't instantly see everything through the lens of self-destruction, I'm trying to reframe how I think of what the nun said. I sometimes reflect on that conversation when I'm alone and walking my dog for miles. I wonder if perhaps I can find a way to view living with illness, rather than dying because of it, as my deepest and most meaningful prayer.

ACKNOWLEDGMENTS

The manuscript for this book was developed over many years, most of it while I was still working. During that time a number of friends read the text and gave me their comments. I appreciate all the input I received from Jerry Gough, Joe Ruth, Sharon Rogers, Sarah Hollister, Emily Dibble, Armand Larive, Barb Kramer, Becky Bitter, Barbara Petur, Jim and Bertie Weddell, Kathleen and Evan Rogers, Ginger Glawe, English and Cindy Pearcy, Anne Dickau, and Ken and Sally Vogel. Before her death, my mother read a draft of the book and gave me comments. Finally, Mary Lauver read the book and shared a home with me while I completed the manuscript, offering me words of encouragement on the race's final lap.

I have always found that writing a book is a group effort. I am humbled by all the help I have received from my community of friends and family. My deepest thanks to all.

Made in the USA
Coppell, TX
11 December 2023